FOR ORGANS, PIANOS & ELECTRONIC KEYBOARDS

Antonio Carlos Jobim

ISBN 978-1-4234-3650-8

7777 W. BLUEMOUND RD. P.O. BOX 13819 MILWAUKEE, WI 53213

Visit Hal Leonard Online at
www.halleonard.com

CONTENTS

Água de Beber
(Water to Drink)

Registration 8
Rhythm: Bossa Nova or Latin

English Words by Norman Gimbel
Portuguese Words by Vinicius de Moraes
Music by Antonio Carlos Jobim

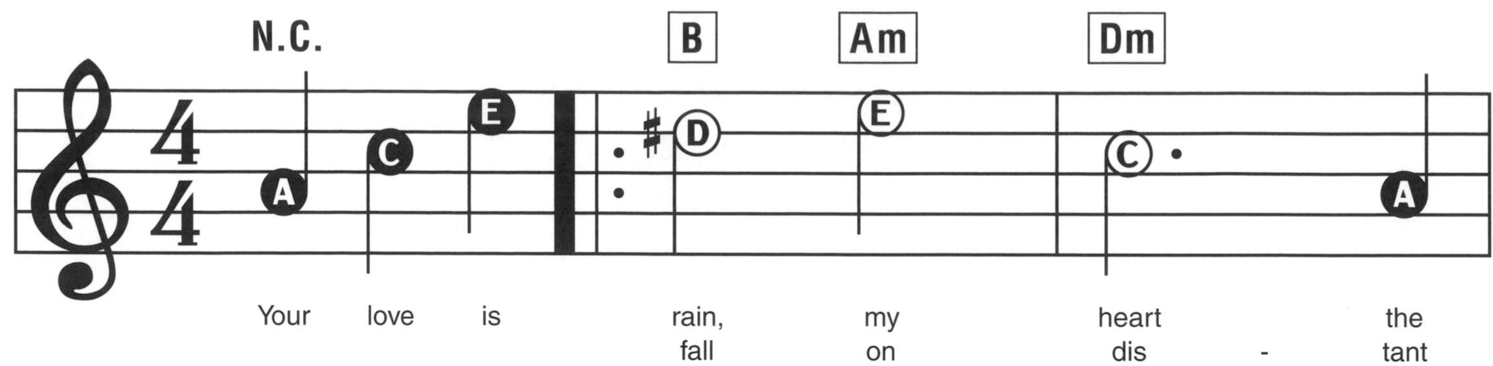

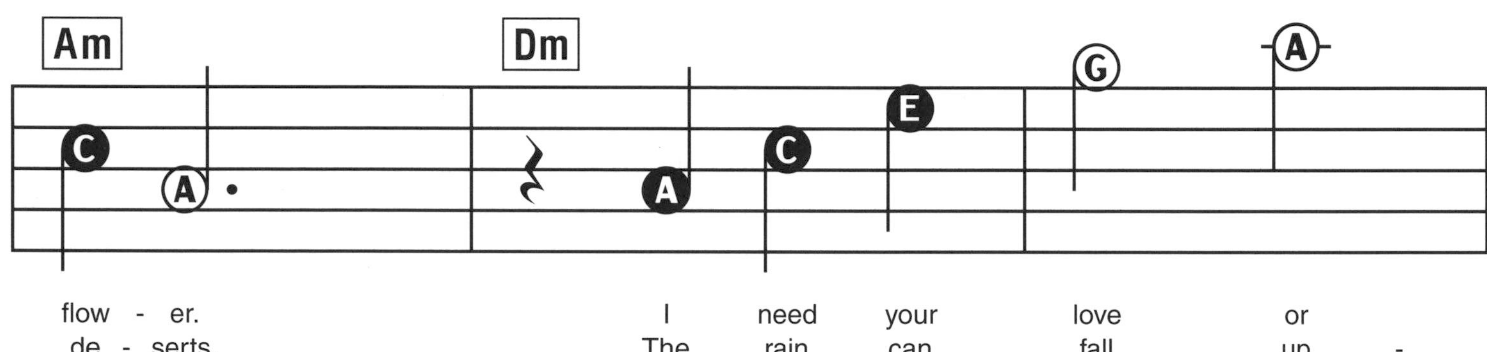

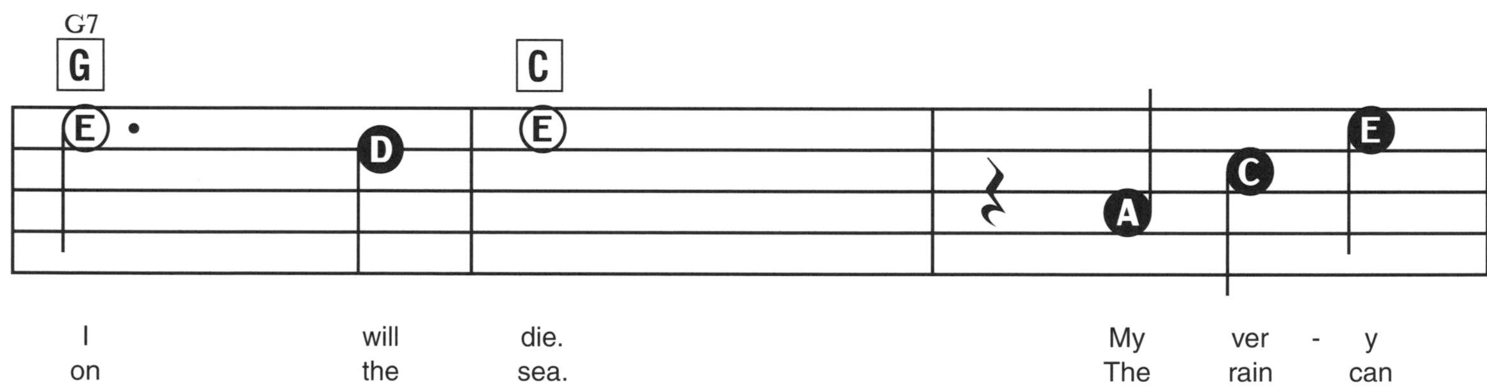

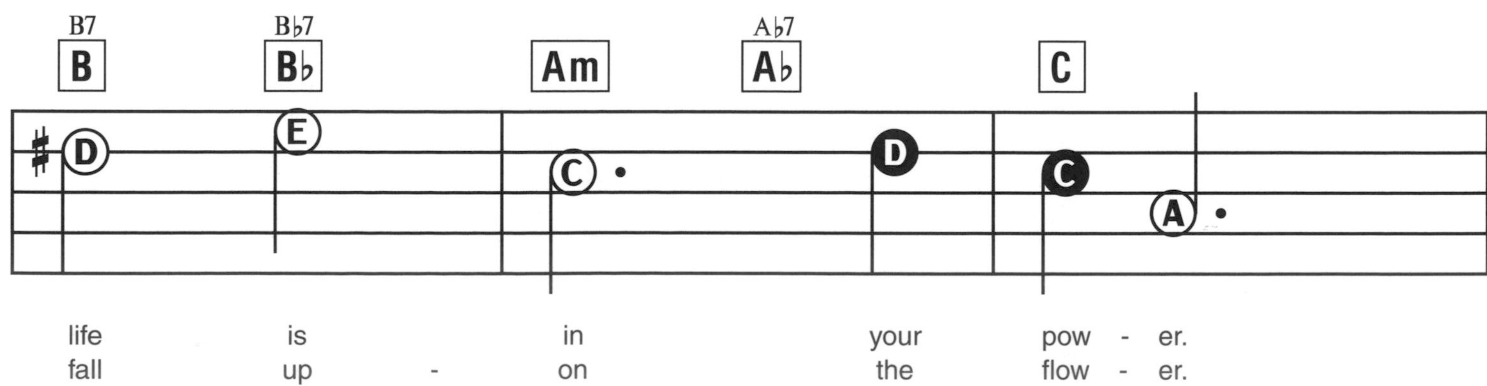

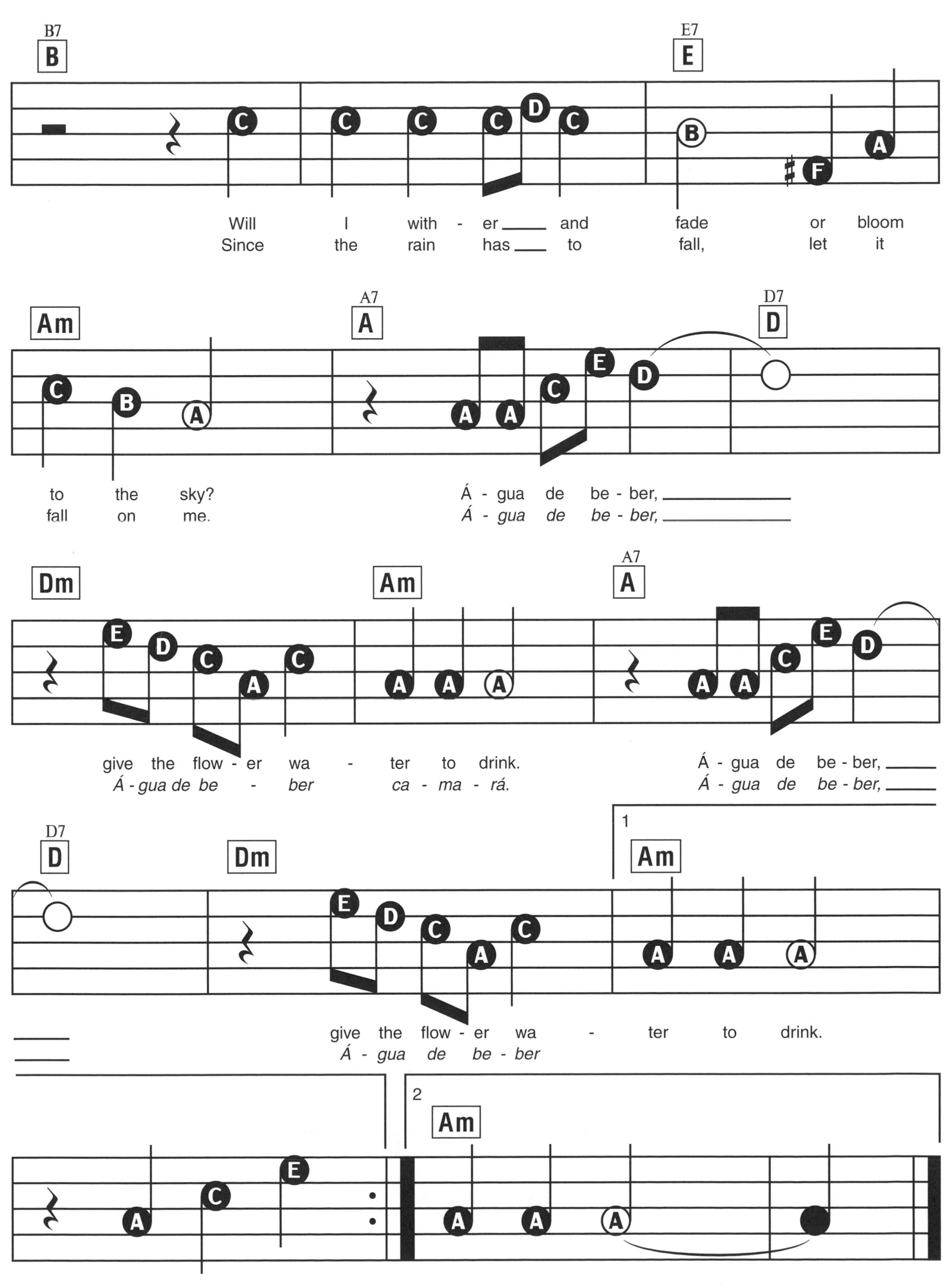
B7
B
E7
E
C
C
C
C
D
C
B
F
A
Will I with - er and fade or bloom
Since the rain has to fall, let it
Am
A7
A
D7
D
C
B
A
A
A
C
E
D
to the sky? Á - gua de be - ber,
fall on me. Á - gua de be - ber,
Dm
Am
A7
A
E
D
C
A
C
A
A
A
A
A
C
E
D
give the flow - er wa - ter to drink. Á - gua de be - ber,
Á - gua de be - ber ca - ma - rá. Á - gua de be - ber,
D7
D
Dm
1
Am
E
D
C
A
C
A
A
A
give the flow - er wa - ter to drink.
Á - gua de be - ber
2
Am
A
C
E
A
A
A
The rain can ca - ma - rá.

Águas de Março
(Waters of March)

Registration 4
Rhythm: Bossa Nova or Latin

Words and Music by
Antonio Carlos Jobim

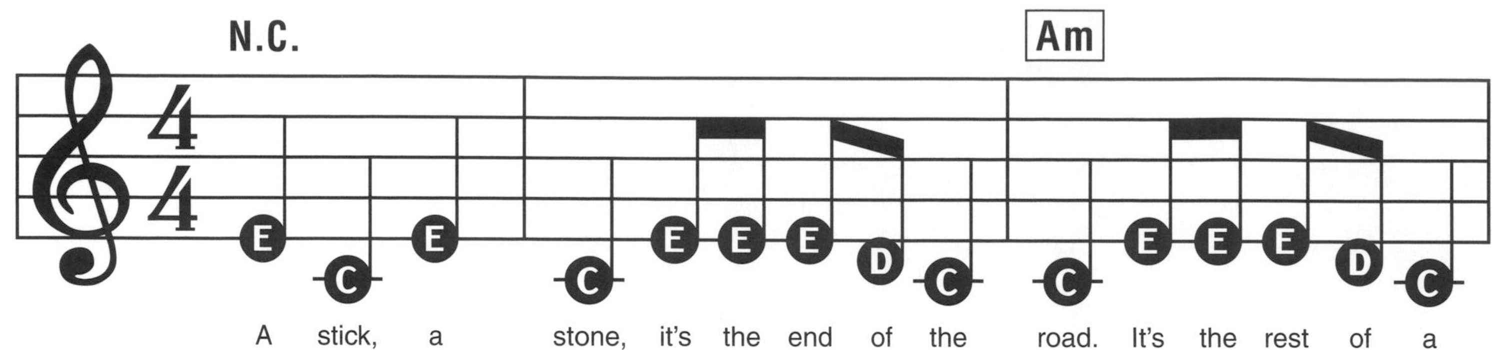

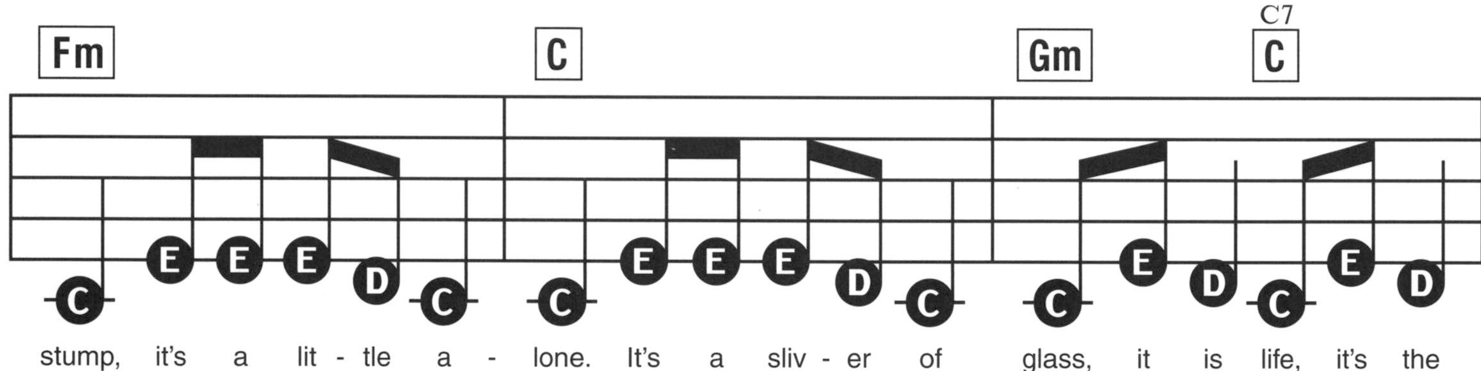

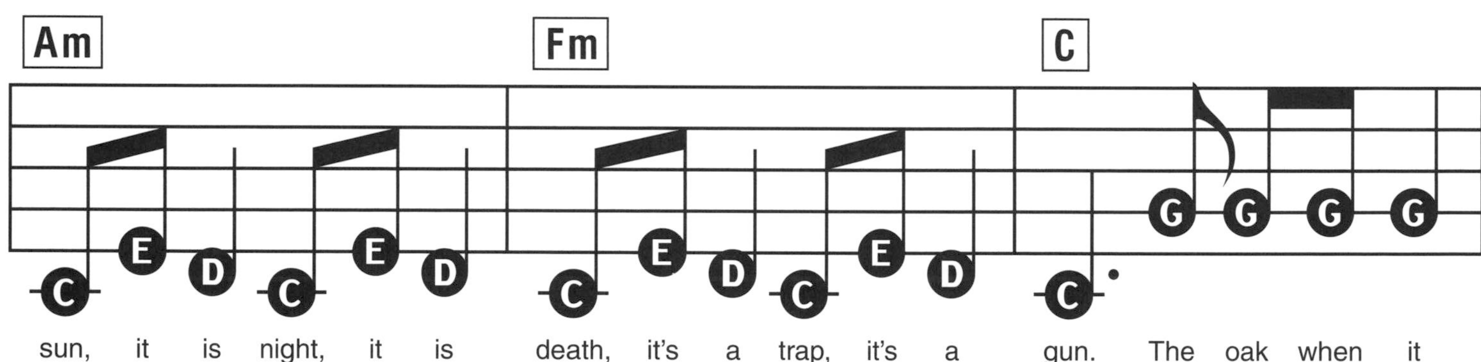

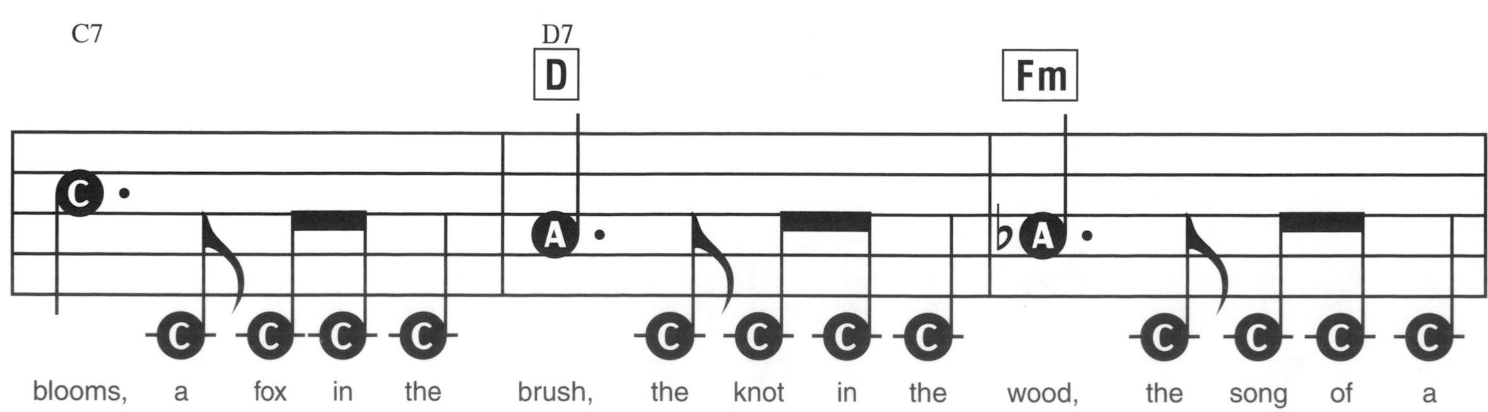

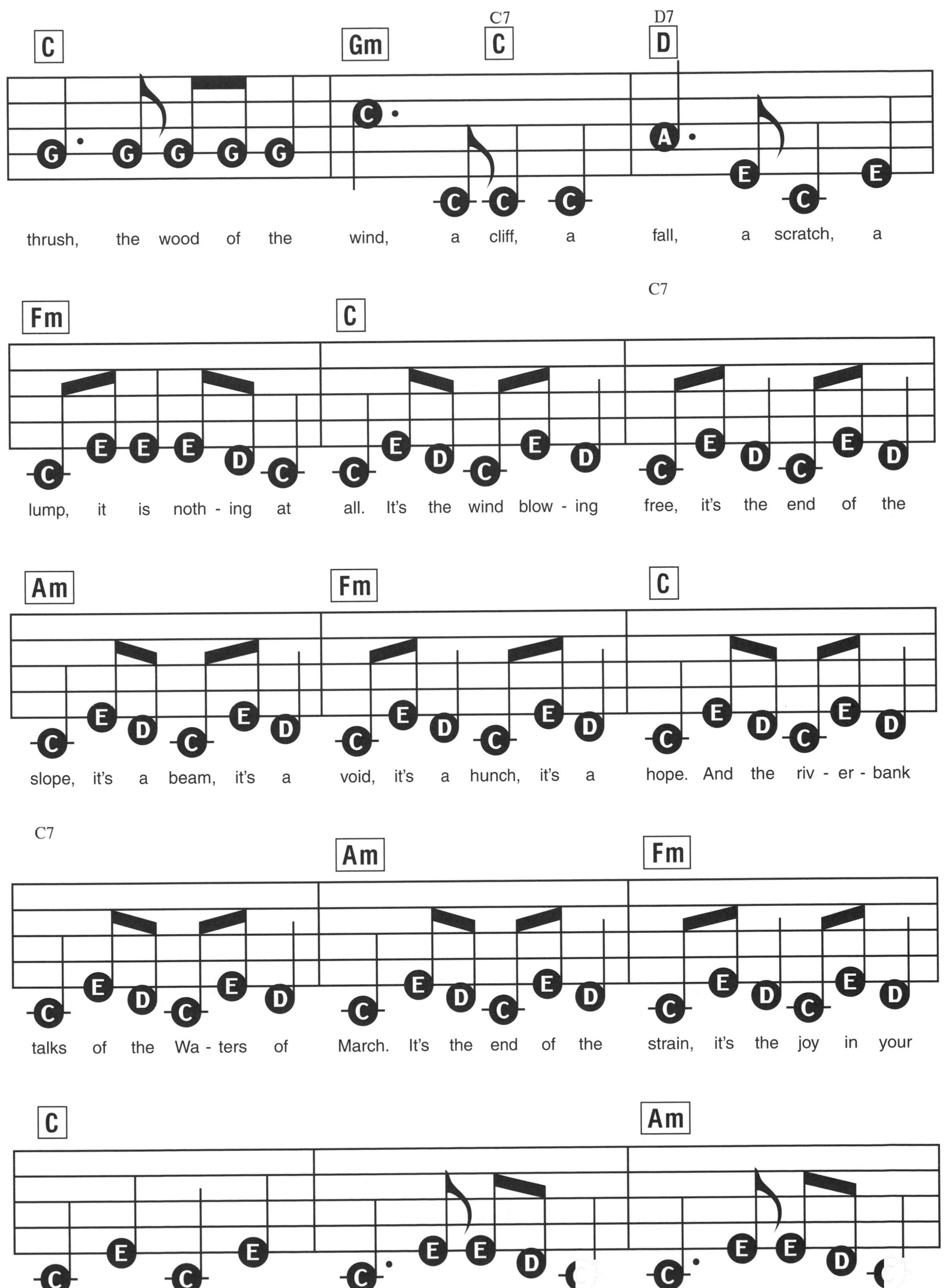
C Gm C7 C D7 D
thrush, the wood of the wind, a cliff, a fall, a scratch, a
Fm C C7
lump, it is noth - ing at all. It's the wind blow - ing free, it's the end of the
Am Fm C
slope, it's a beam, it's a void, it's a hunch, it's a hope. And the riv - er - bank
C7 Am Fm
talks of the Wa - ters of March. It's the end of the strain, it's the joy in your
C Am
heart. The foot, the ground, the flesh and the bone, the beat of the

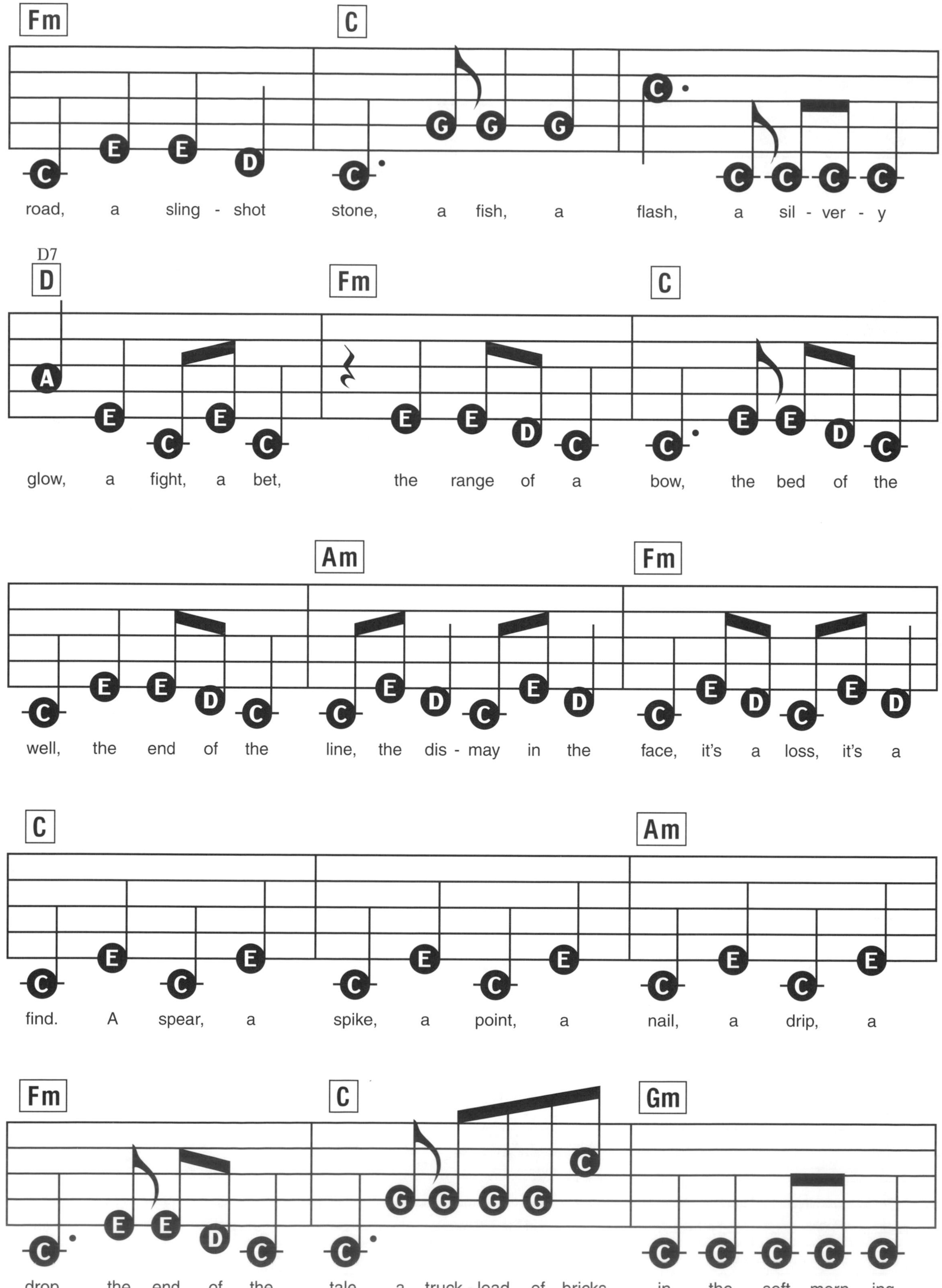
Fm
C
road, a sling - shot stone, a fish, a flash, a sil - ver - y
D7
D
Fm
C
glow, a fight, a bet, the range of a bow, the bed of the
Am
Fm
well, the end of the line, the dis - may in the face, it's a loss, it's a
C
Am
find. A spear, a spike, a point, a nail, a drip, a
Fm
C
Gm
drop, the end of the tale, a truck - load of bricks in the soft morn - ing

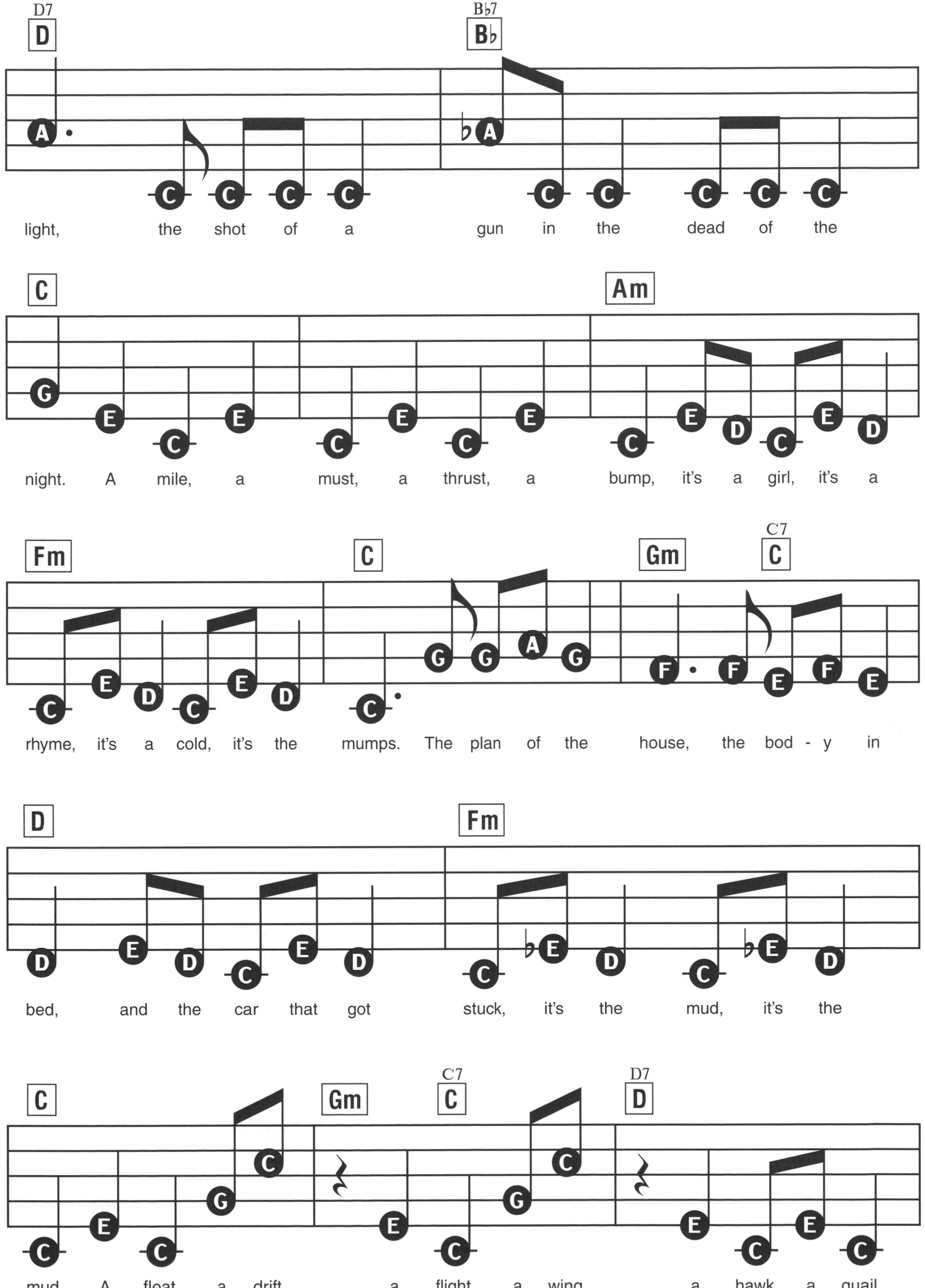
D7
D
B♭7
B♭
light, the shot of a gun in the dead of the
C
Am
night. A mile, a must, a thrust, a bump, it's a girl, it's a
Fm
C
Gm
C7
C
rhyme, it's a cold, it's the mumps. The plan of the house, the bod - y in
D
Fm
bed, and the car that got stuck, it's the mud, it's the
C
Gm
C7
C
D7
D
mud. A float, a drift, a flight, a wing, a hawk, a quail,

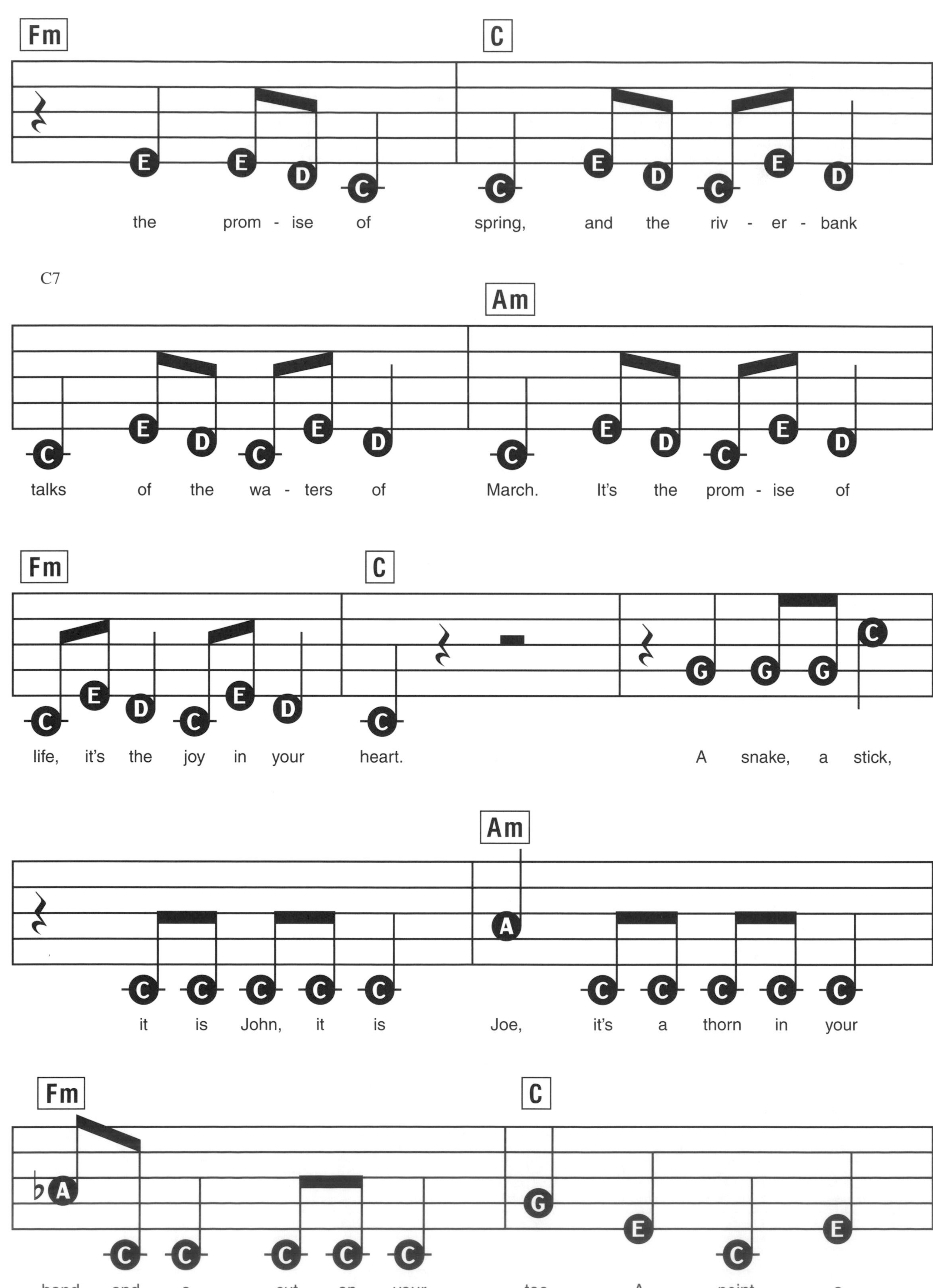
Fm
C
E E D C
C E D C E D
the prom - ise of
spring, and the riv - er - bank
C7
Am
C E D C E D
C E D C E D
talks of the wa - ters of
March. It's the prom - ise of
Fm
C
C E D C E D
C
G G G C
life, it's the joy in your
heart.
A snake, a stick,
Am
C C C C C
A C C C C C
it is John, it is
Joe, it's a thorn in your
Fm
C
A C C C C C
G E C E
hand, and a cut on your
toe. A point, a

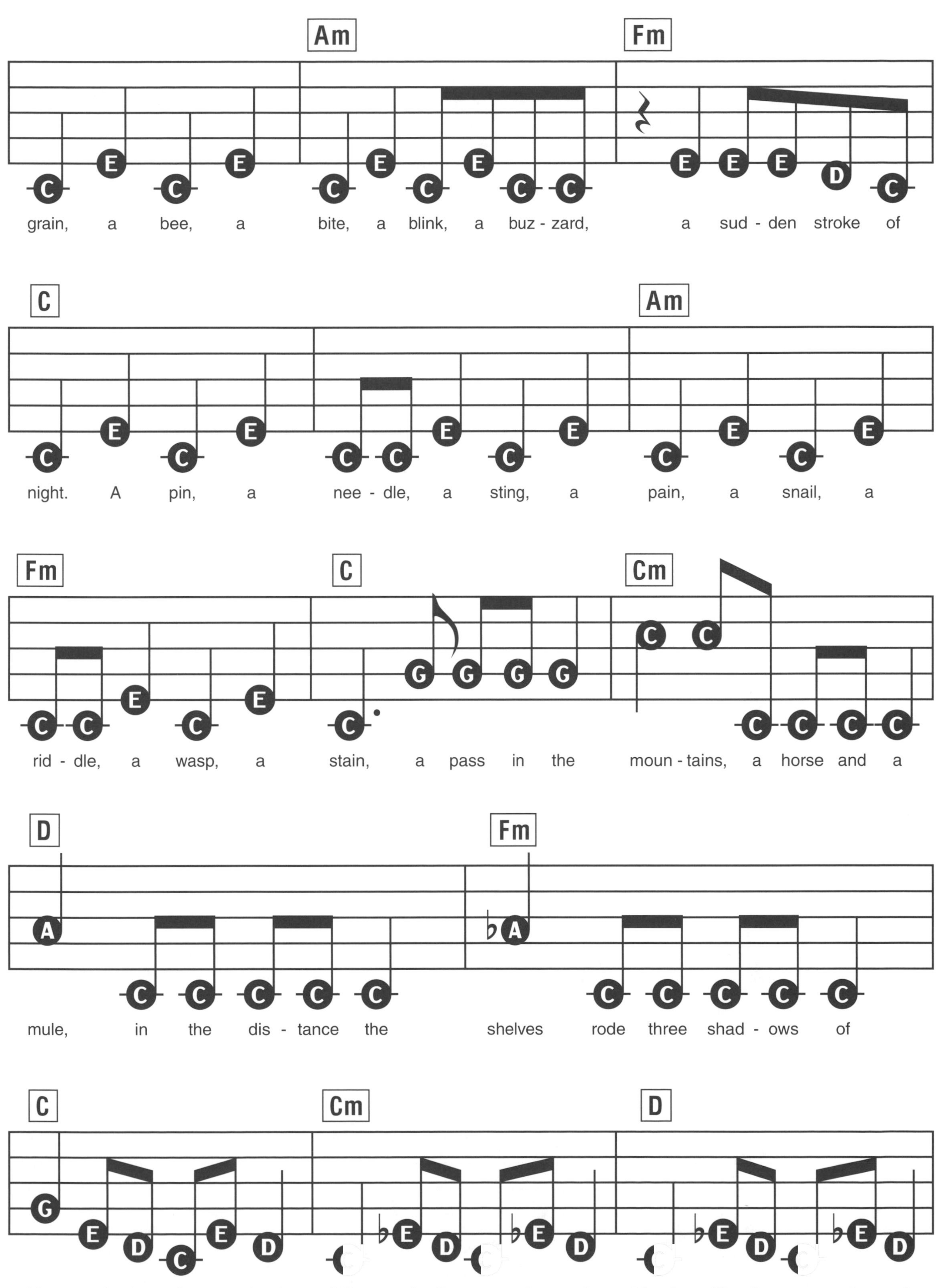
Am
Fm
grain, a bee, a bite, a blink, a buz - zard, a sud - den stroke of
C
Am
night. A pin, a nee - dle, a sting, a pain, a snail, a
Fm
C
Cm
rid - dle, a wasp, a stain, a pass in the moun - tains, a horse and a
D
Fm
mule, in the dis - tance the shelves rode three shad - ows of
C
Cm
D
blue, and the riv - er - bank talks of the wa - ters of March. It's the prom - ise of

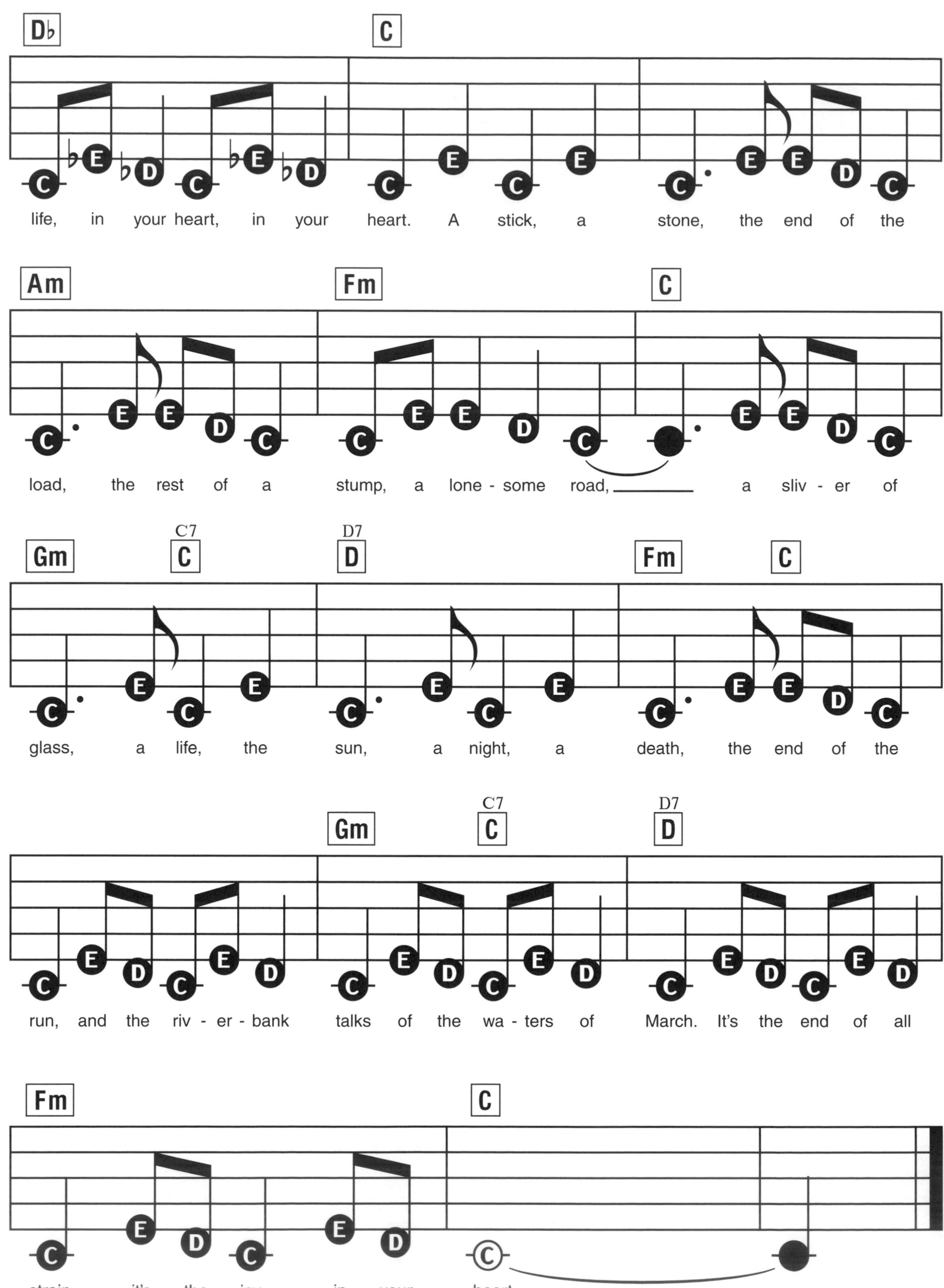
D♭
C
life, in your heart, in your heart. A stick, a stone, the end of the
Am
Fm
C
load, the rest of a stump, a lone - some road, a sliv - er of
Gm
C7
C
D7
D
Fm
C
glass, a life, the sun, a night, a death, the end of the
Gm
C7
C
D7
D
run, and the riv - er - bank talks of the wa - ters of March. It's the end of all
Fm
C
strain, it's the joy in your heart.

Dindi

Registration 4
Rhythm: Bossa Nova or Latin

Music by Antonio Carlos Jobim
Portuguese Lyrics by Aloysio de Oliveira
English Lyrics by Ray Gilbert

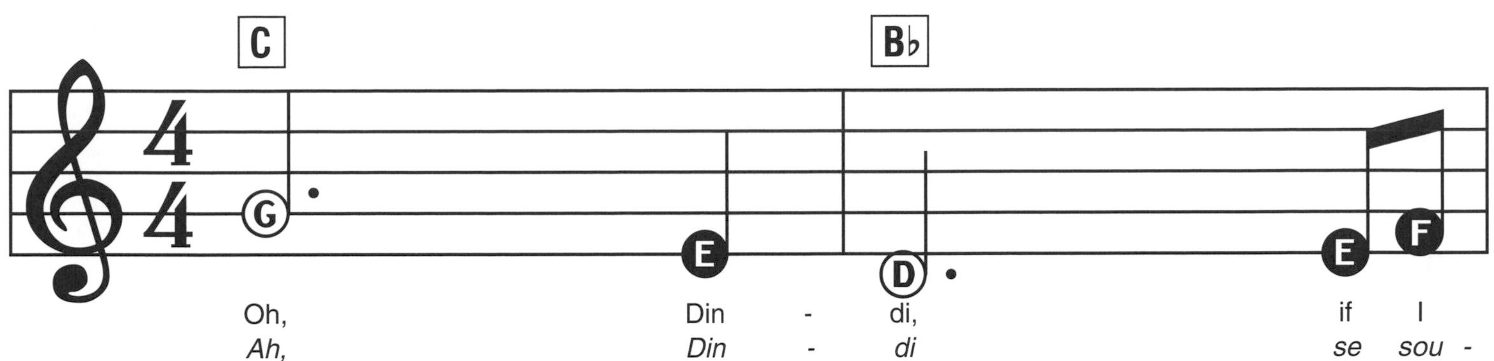

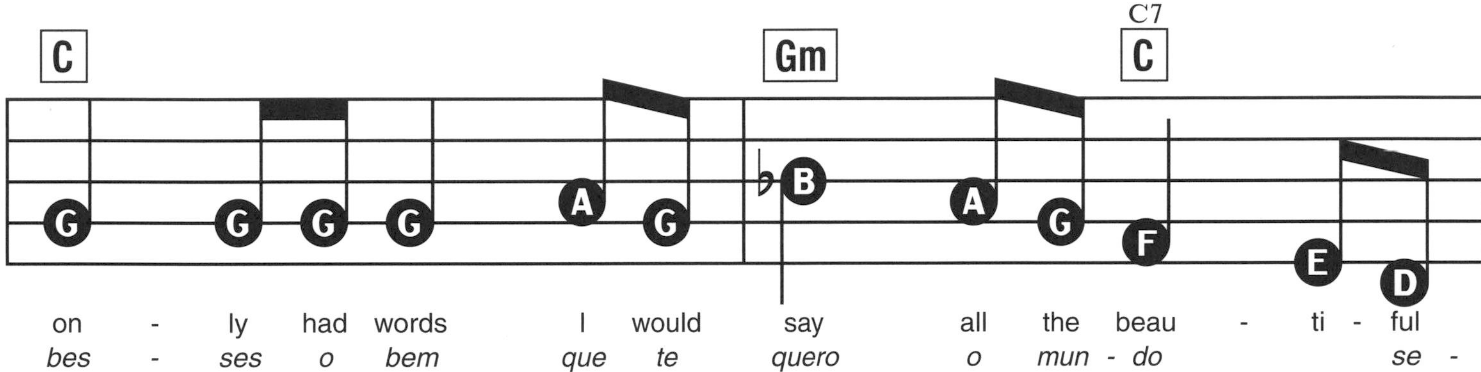

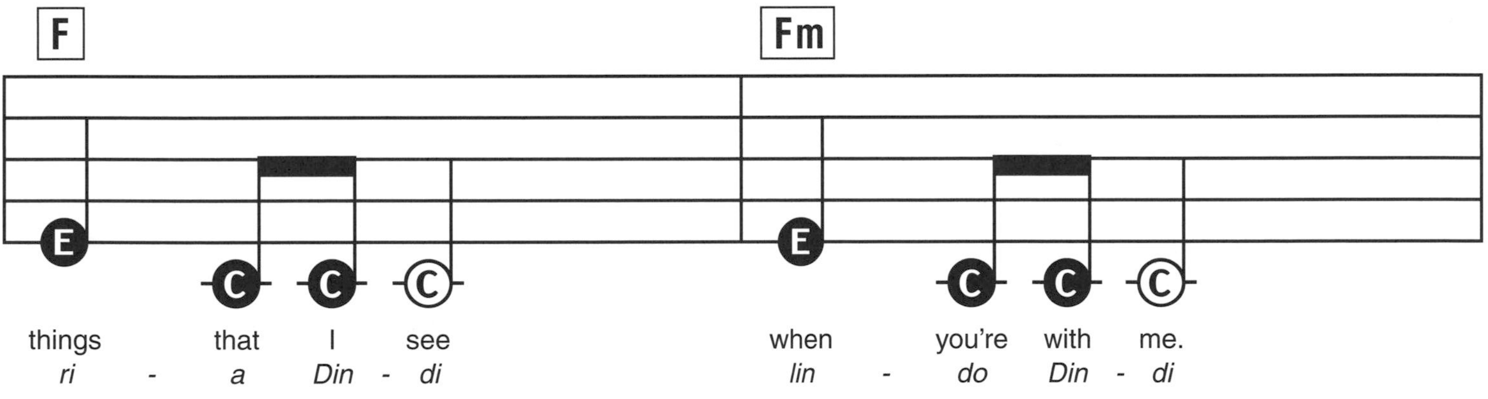

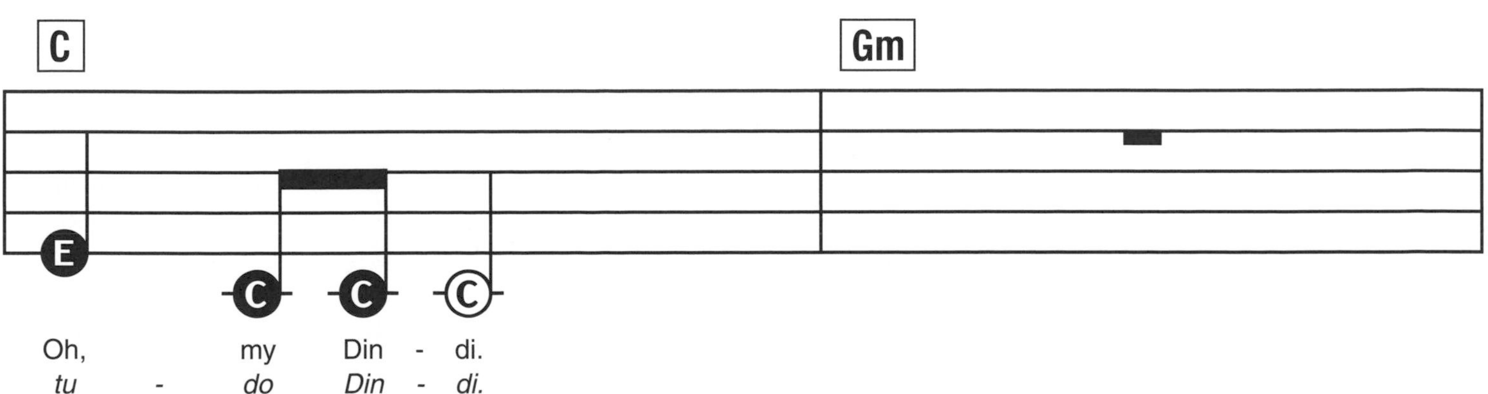

C
B♭
C
Oh, Din - di, like the song of the wind in the
Ah, Din - di se um dia vo - ce for em - bora
Gm
C7
C
F
trees, that's how my heart is sing - ing, Din - di
nie la - va con - ti - go Din - di
Fm
C
hap - py Din - di, when you're with me.
fi - ca, Din - di, Ol - ha Din - di.
B7
B
Em
I love you more each
E as a - guas deste
Cm
Em
Cm
Em
A7
A
day, yes, I do, yes, I do.
rio On - de vâo, eu nâo sei,

Dm
B♭m
I'd let you go a - way
A mi - nha vi - da inteira,
if you
es - per -
Dm
B♭m
Dm
G7
G
C
take me with you.
ei, es - per - ei
Don't you know, Din -
Por vo - ce Din -
B♭
C
di, I'd be run - ning and search - ing for
di Que é a coi - sa mais lin - da que
Gm
C7
C
F
you like a riv - er that can't find the sea,
e - xis - te vo - ce nao e - xiste Din - di
B♭7
B♭
C
that would be me with - out you, my Din - di.
Dei - xa Din - di que eu te a - dore Din - di.

Chega de Saudade
(No More Blues)

Registration 4
Rhythm: Bossa Nova or Latin

English Lyric by Jon Hendricks
and Jessie Cavanaugh
Original Text by Vinicius de Moraes
Music by Antonio Carlos Jobim

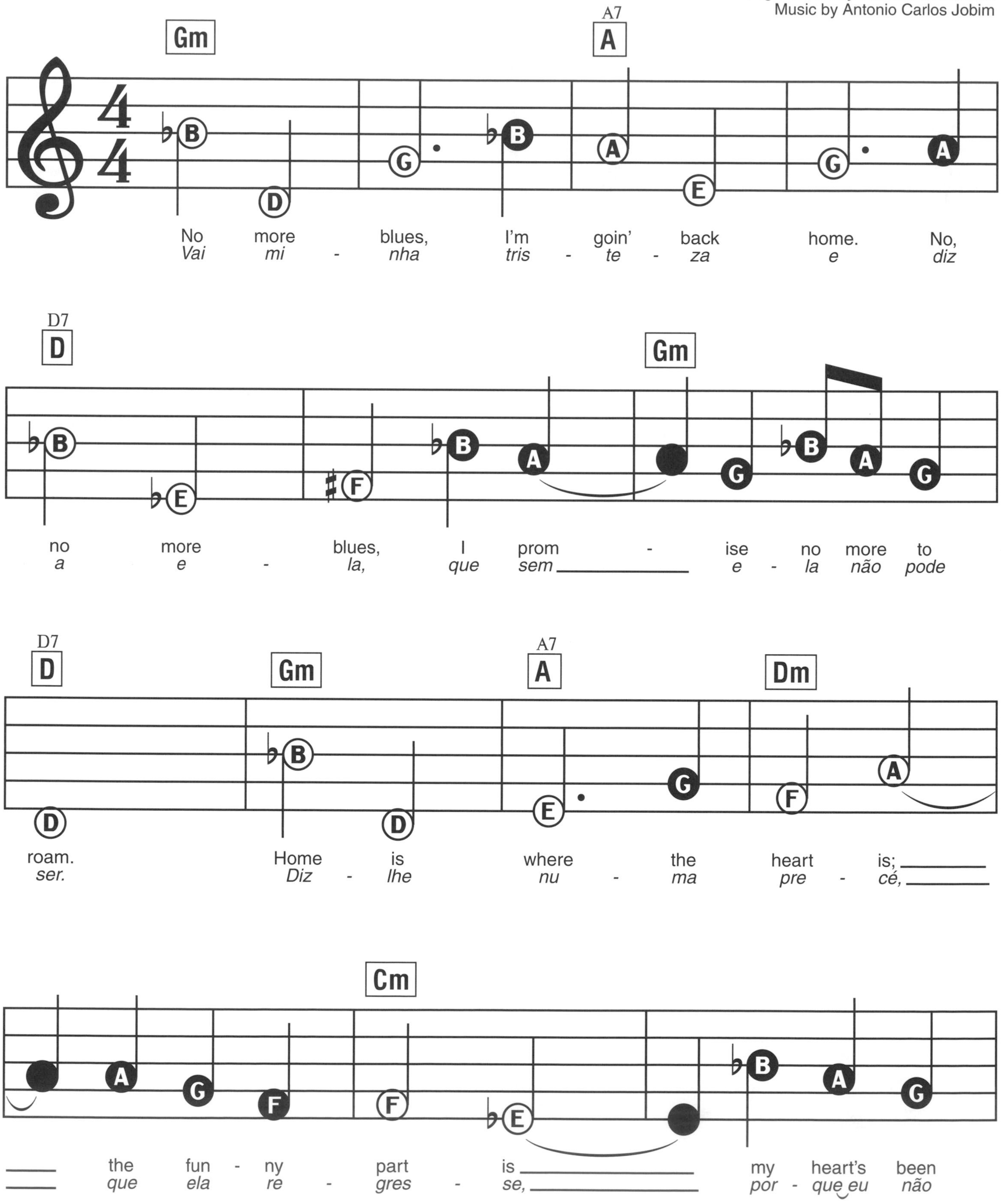

Gm A7 A

No more blues, I'm goin' back home. No,
Vai mi - nha tris - te - za e diz

D7 D Gm

no more blues, I prom - ise no more to
a e - la, que sem e - la não pode

D7 D Gm A7 A Dm

roam. Home is where the heart is;
ser. Diz - lhe nu - ma pre - cé,

Cm

the fun - ny part is my heart's been
que ela re - gres - se, por - que eu não

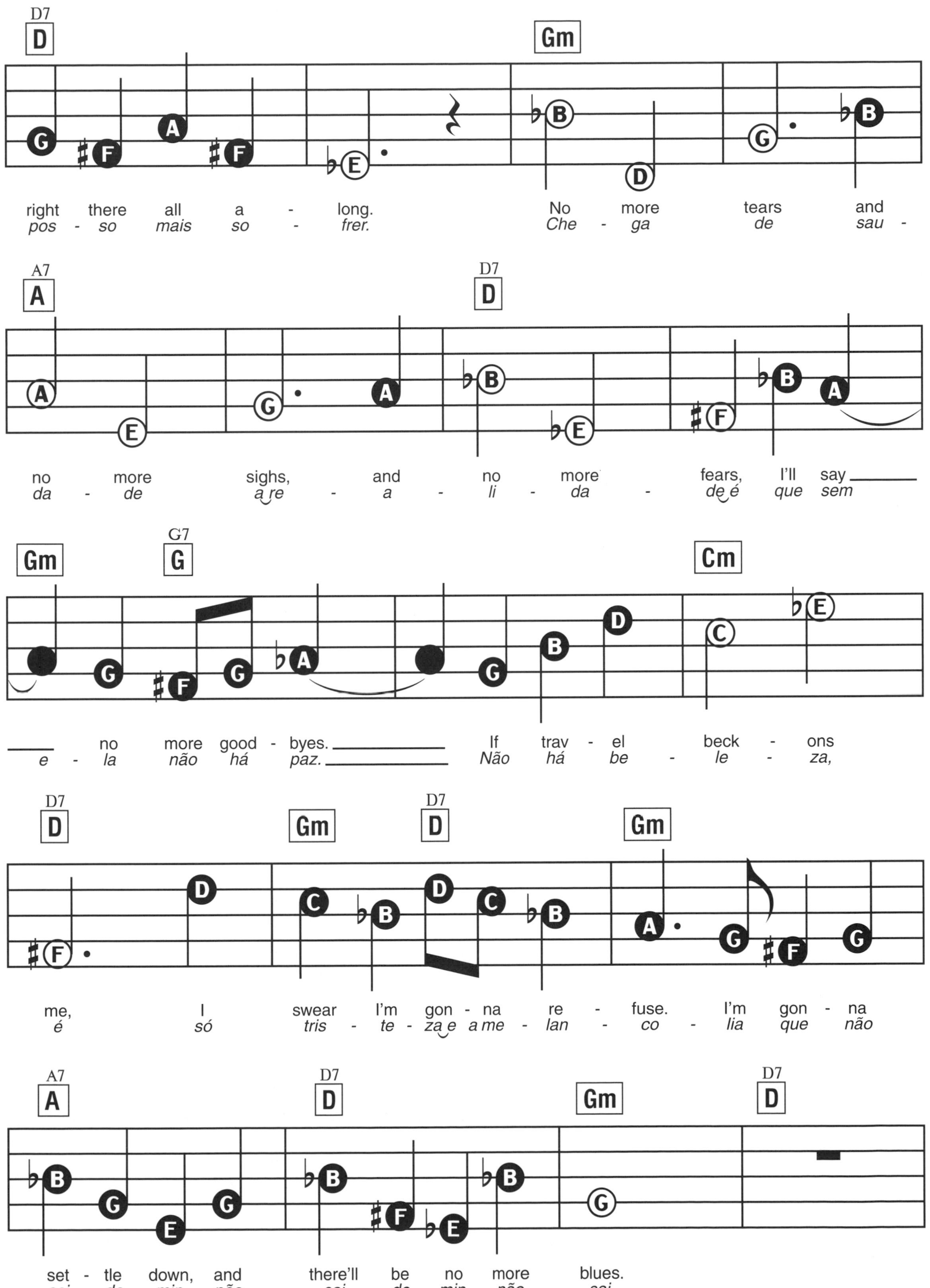
D7
D
Gm
right there all a - long.
pos - so mais so - frer.
No more tears and
Che - ga de sau -
A7
A
D7
D
no more sighs, and no more fears, I'll say
da - de a re - a - li - da - de é que sem
Gm
G7
G
Cm
no more good - byes. If trav - el beck - ons
e - la não há paz. Não há be - le - za,
D7
D
Gm
D7
D
Gm
me, I swear I'm gon - na re - fuse. I'm gon - na
é só tris - te - za e a me - lan - co - lia que não
A7
A
D7
D
Gm
D7
D
set - tle down, and there'll be no more blues.
sai de min, não sai de min, não sai.

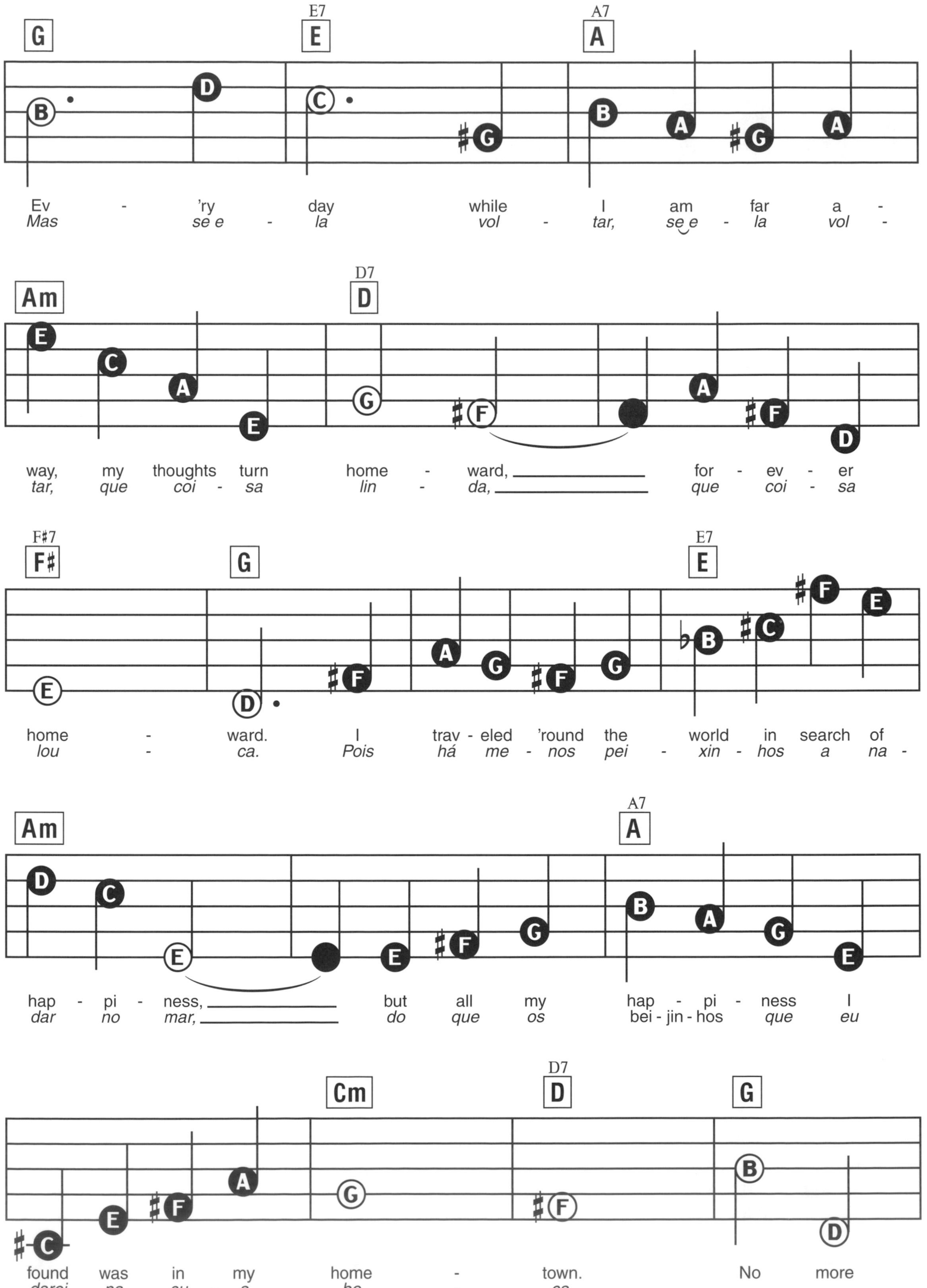
G
E7 E
A7 A
Ev - 'ry day while I am far a -
Mas se e - la vol - tar, se e - la vol -
Am
D7 D
way, my thoughts turn home - ward, for - ev - er
tar, que coi - sa lin - da, que coi - sa
F♯7 F♯
G
E7 E
home - ward. I trav - eled 'round the world in search of
lou - ca. Pois há me - nos pei - xin - hos a na -
Am
A7 A
hap - pi - ness, but all my hap - pi - ness I
dar no mar, do que os bei - jin - hos que eu
Cm
D7 D
G
found was in my home - town. No more
darei na su - a bo - ca.

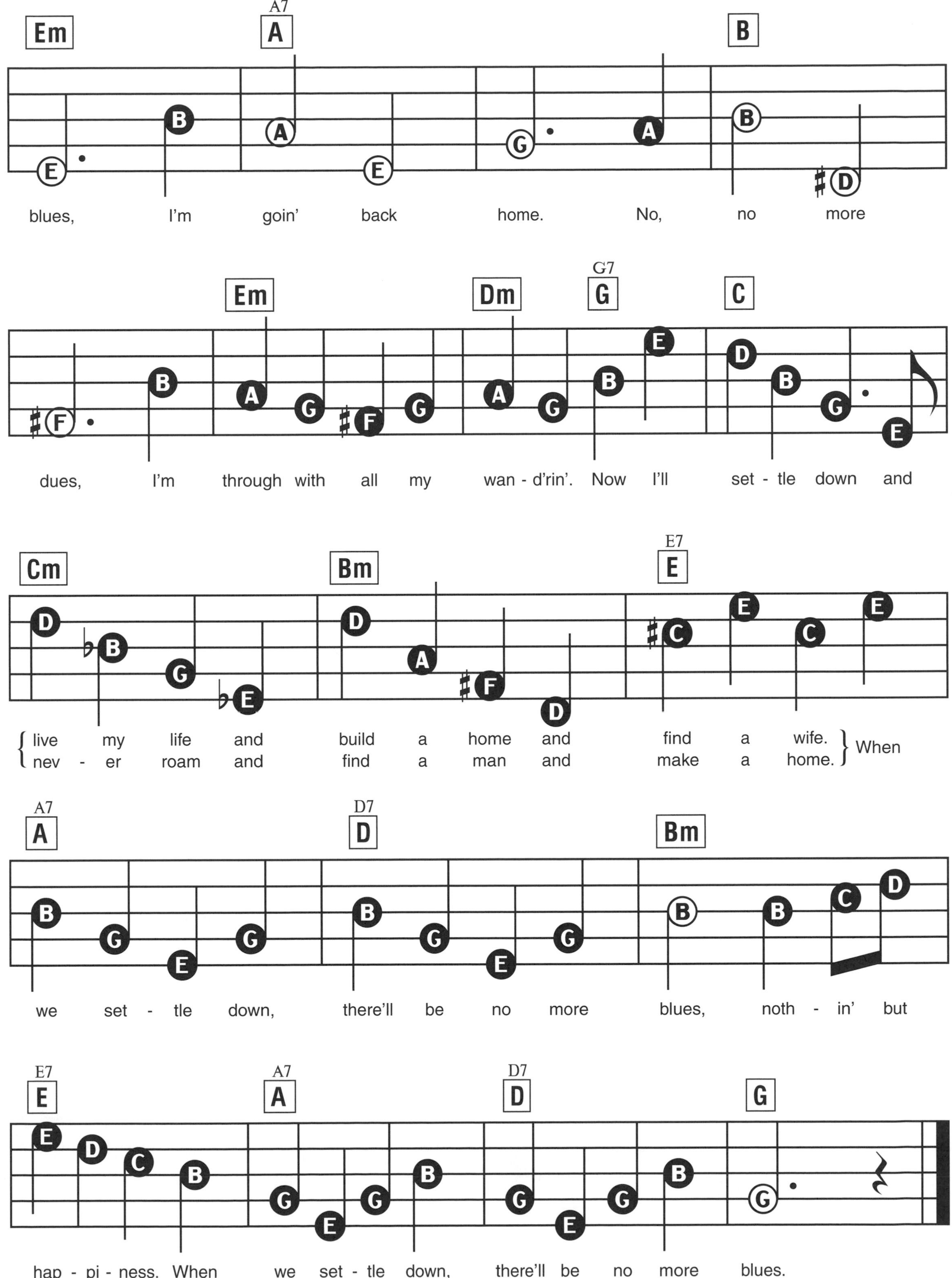
Em
A7
A
B
blues, I'm goin' back home. No, no more
Em
Dm
G7
G
C
dues, I'm through with all my wan - d'rin'. Now I'll set - tle down and
Cm
Bm
E7
E
live my life and build a home and find a wife.
nev - er roam and find a man and make a home.
When
A7
A
D7
D
Bm
we set - tle down, there'll be no more blues, noth - in' but
E7
E
A7
A
D7
D
G
hap - pi - ness. When we set - tle down, there'll be no more blues.

Desafinado
(Off Key)

Registration 1
Rhythm: Bossa Nova or Latin

English Lyric by Gene Lees
Original Text by Newton Mendonca
Music by Antonio Carlos Jobim

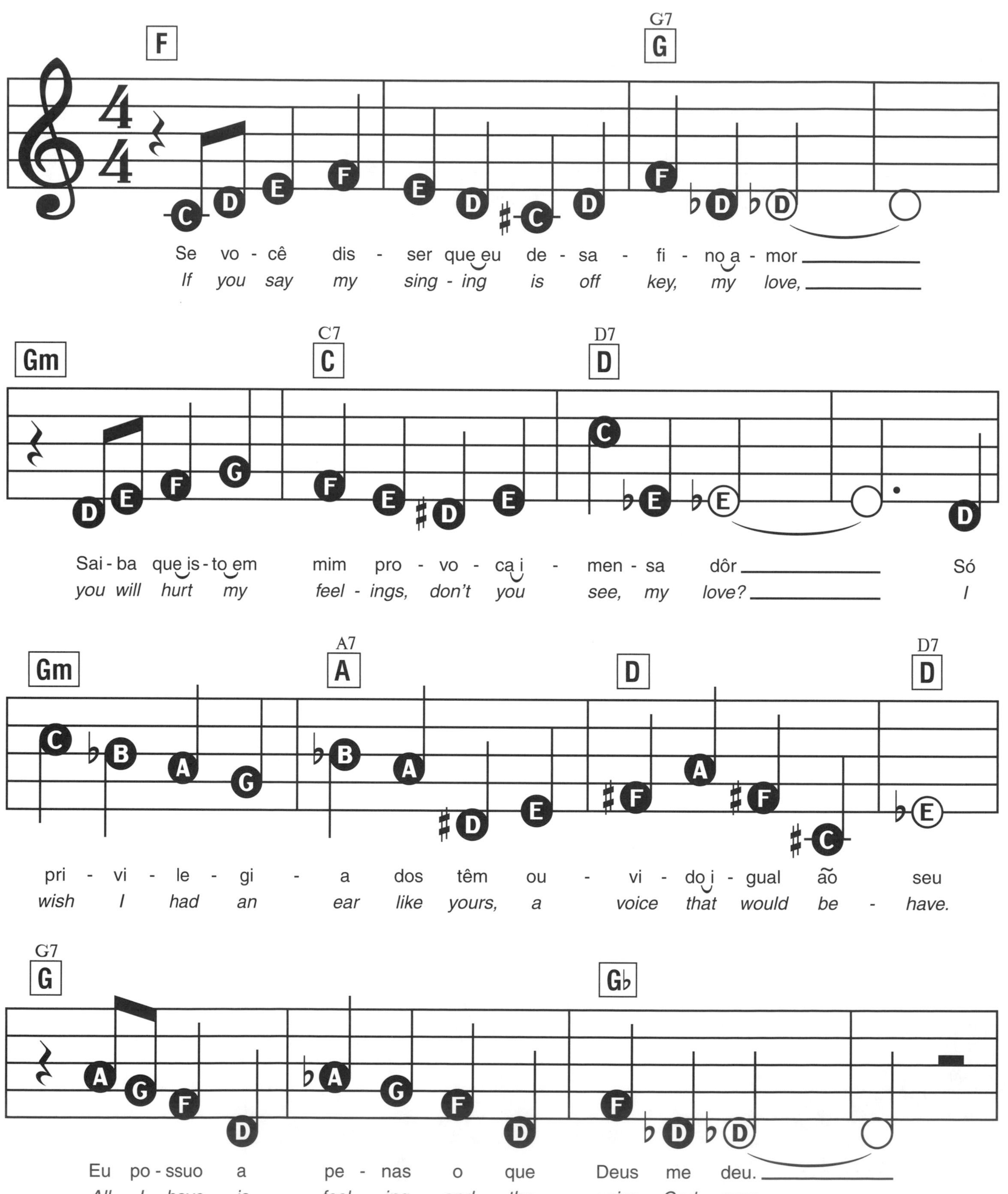

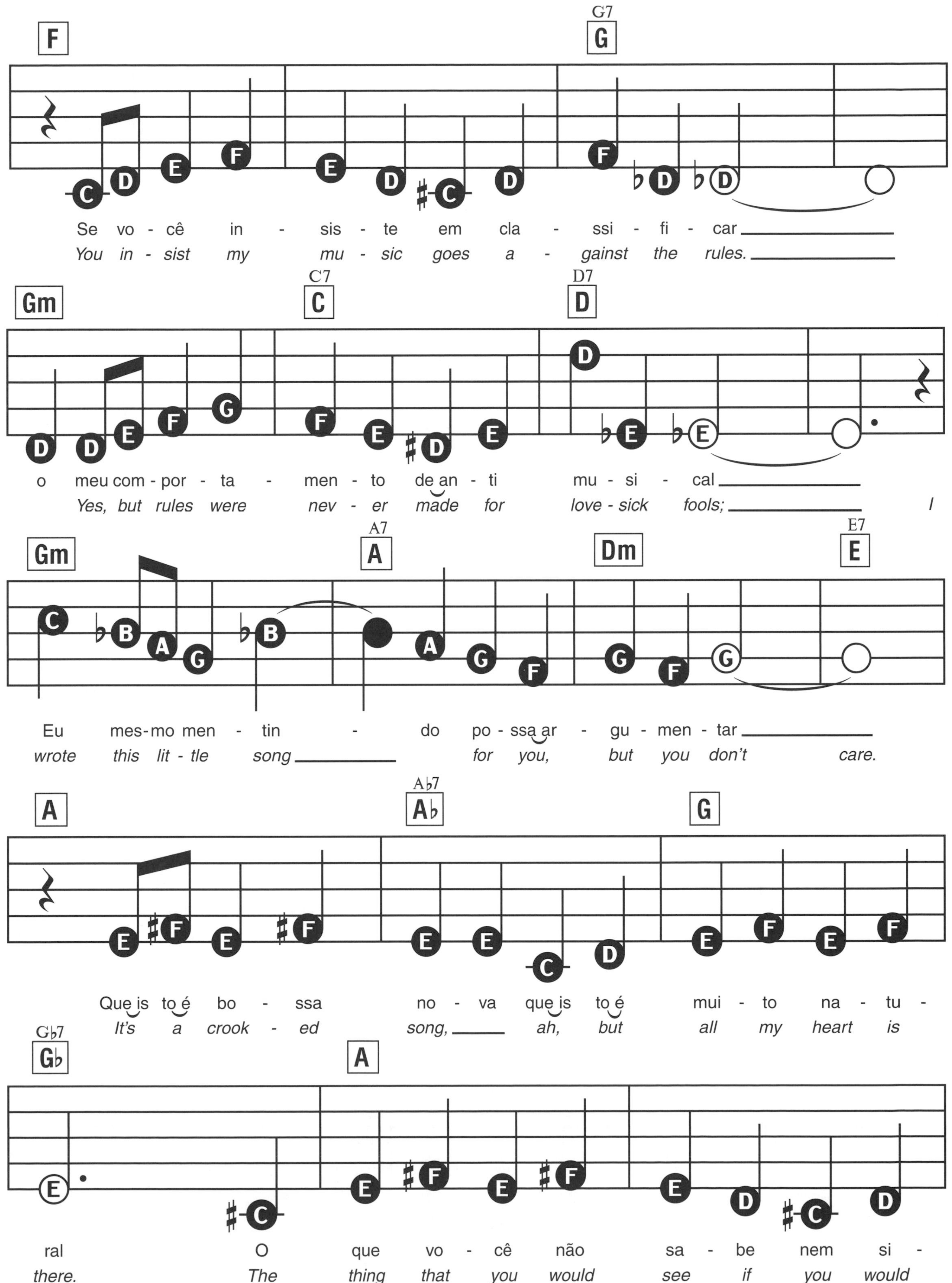
F
G7
G
Se vo - cê in - sis - te em cla - ssi - fi - car
You in - sist my mu - sic goes a - gainst the rules.
Gm
C7
C
D7
D
o meu com - por - ta - men - to de an - ti mu - si - cal
Yes, but rules were nev - er made for love - sick fools; I
Gm
A7
A
Dm
E7
E
Eu mes - mo men - tin - do po - ssa ar - gu - men - tar
wrote this lit - tle song for you, but you don't care.
A
A♭7
A♭
G
Que is to é bo - ssa no - va que is to é mui - to na - tu -
It's a crook - ed song, ah, but all my heart is
G♭7
G♭
A
ral O que vo - cê não sa - be nem si -
there. The thing that you would see if you would

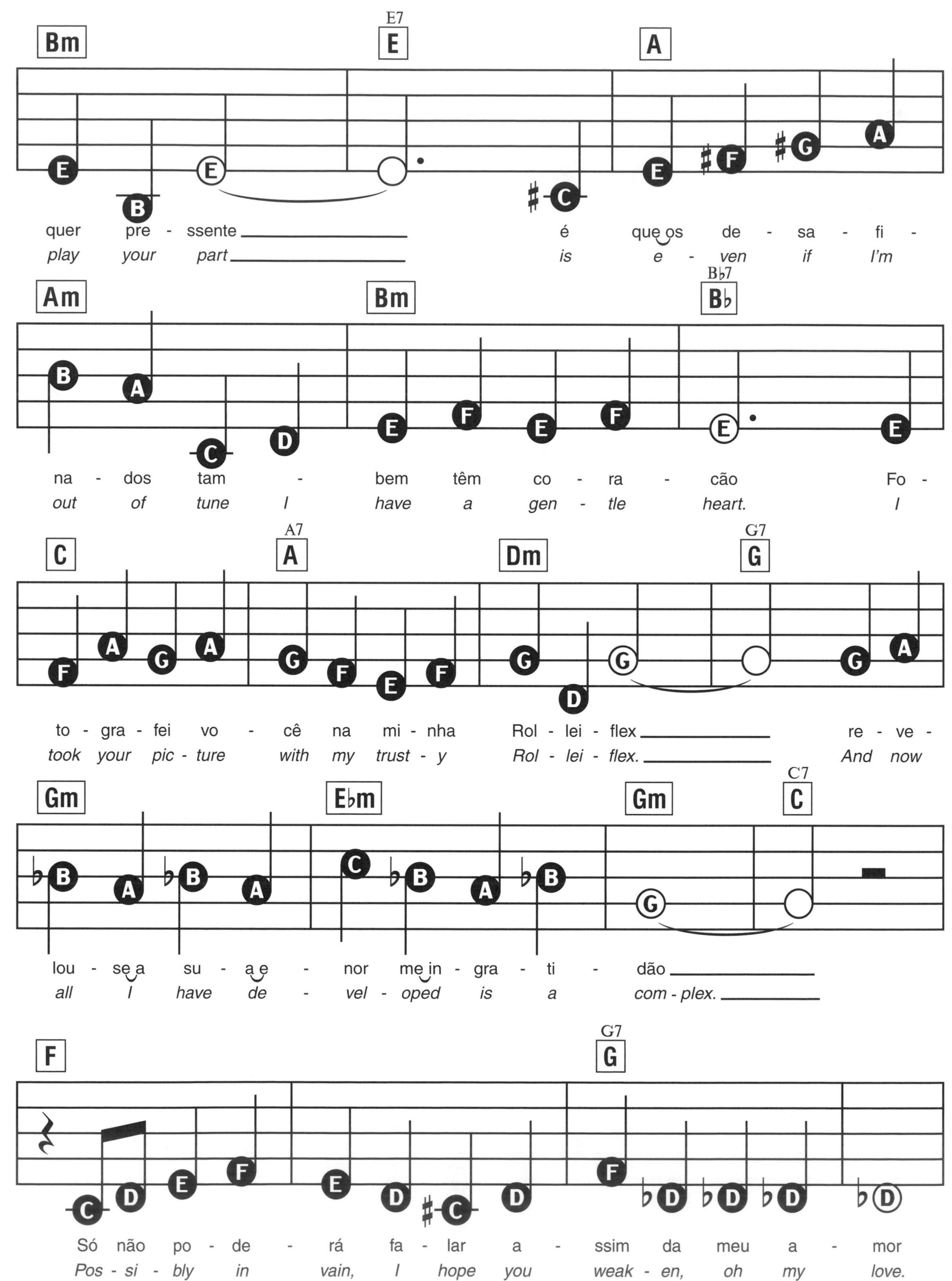
Bm
E7 E
A
quer pre - ssente é que os de - sa - fi -
play your part is e - ven if I'm
Am
Bm
B♭7 B♭
na - dos tam - bem têm co - ra - cão Fo -
out of tune I have a gen - tle heart. I
C
A7 A
Dm
G7 G
to - gra - fei vo - cê na mi - nha Rol - lei - flex re - ve -
took your pic - ture with my trust - y Rol - lei - flex. And now
Gm
E♭m
Gm
C7 C
lou - se a su - a e - nor me in - gra - ti - dão
all I have de - vel - oped is a com - plex.
F
G7 G
Só não po - de - rá fa - lar a - ssim da meu a - mor
Pos - si - bly in vain, I hope you weak - en, oh my love.

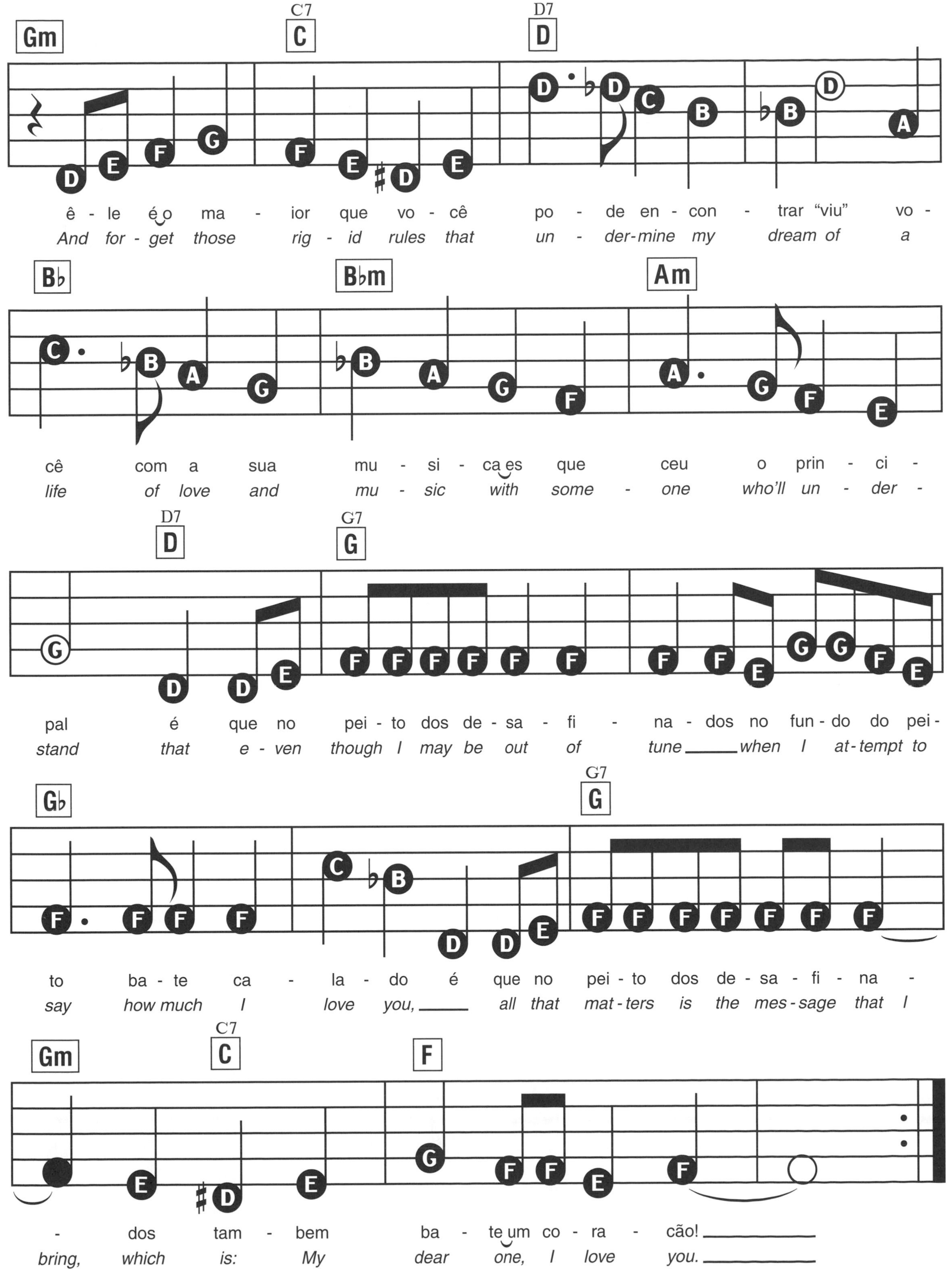
Gm
C7 C
D7 D
ê - le é o ma - ior que vo - cê po - de en - con - trar "viu" vo -
And for - get those rig - id rules that un - der-mine my dream of a
B♭
B♭m
Am
cê com a sua mu - si - ca es que ceu o prin - ci -
life of love and mu - sic with some - one who'll un - der -
D7 D
G7 G
pal é que no pei - to dos de - sa - fi - na - dos no fun - do do pei -
stand that e - ven though I may be out of tune when I at - tempt to
G♭
G7 G
to ba - te ca - la - do é que no pei - to dos de - sa - fi - na -
say how much I love you, all that mat - ters is the mes - sage that I
Gm
C7 C
F
- dos tam - bem ba - te um co - ra - cão!
bring, which is: My dear one, I love you.

A Felicidade

Registration 4
Rhythm: Bossa Nova or Latin

Words and Music by Vinicius de Moraes
and Antonio Carlos Jobim

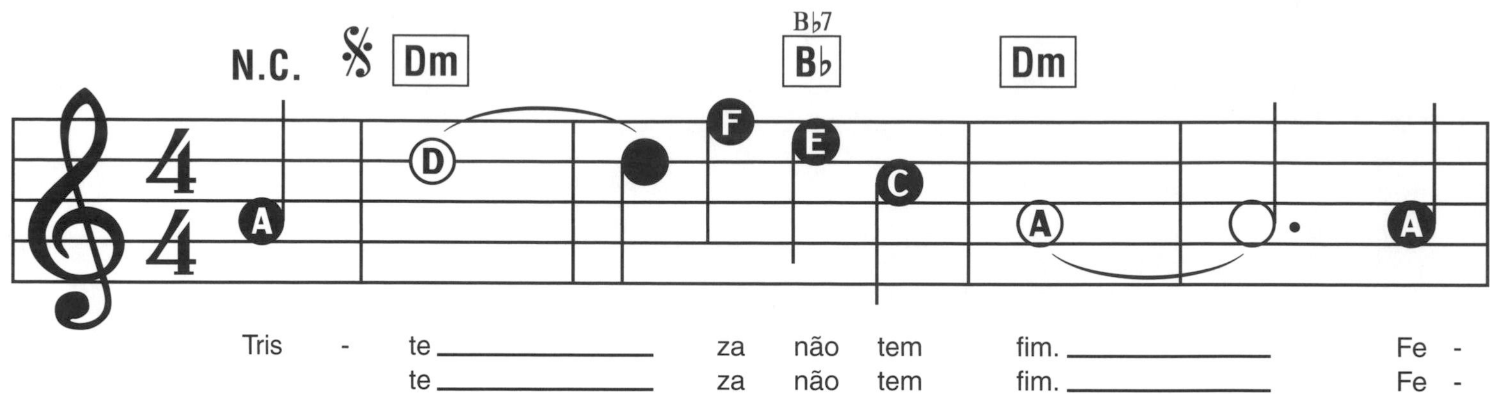

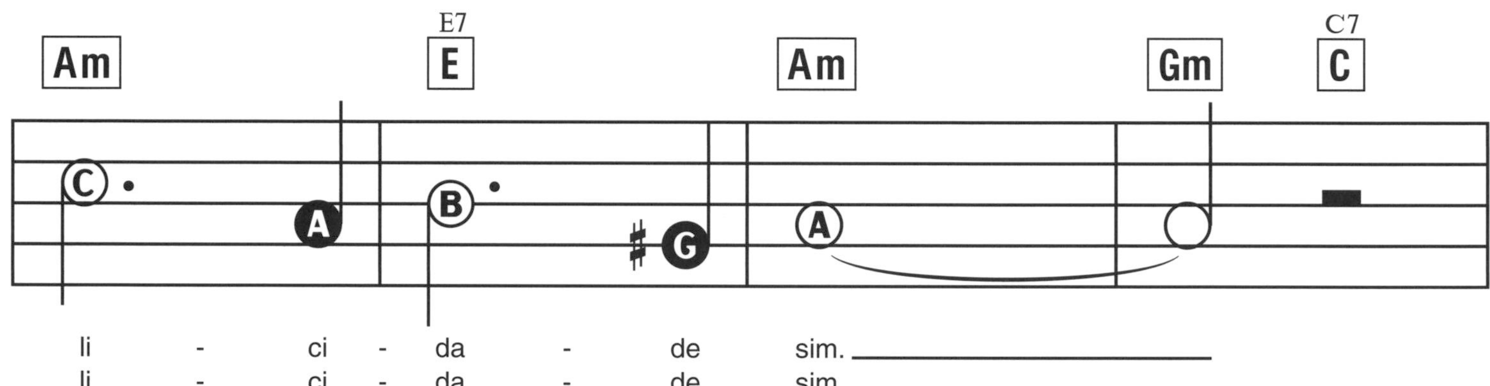

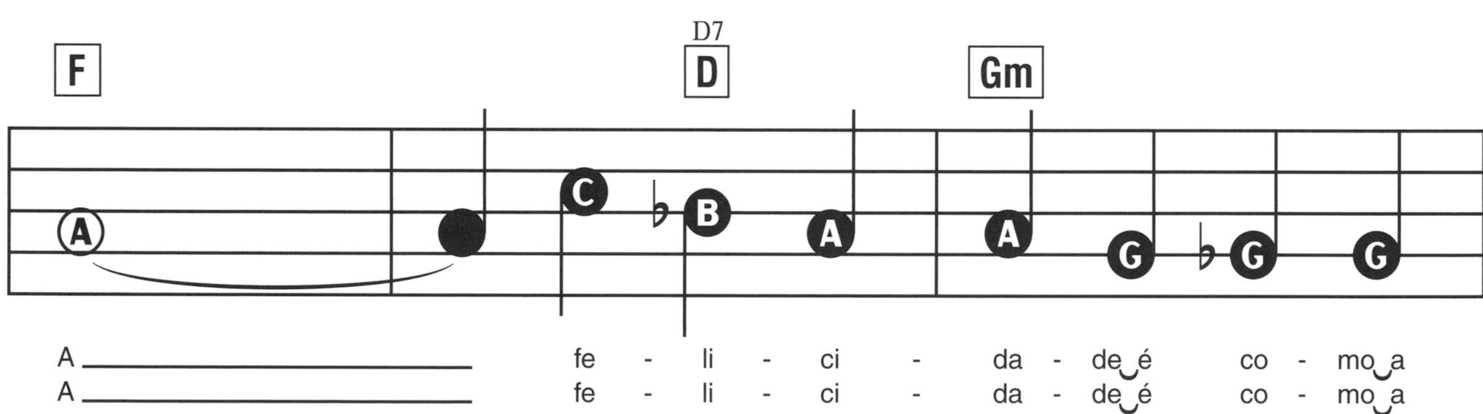

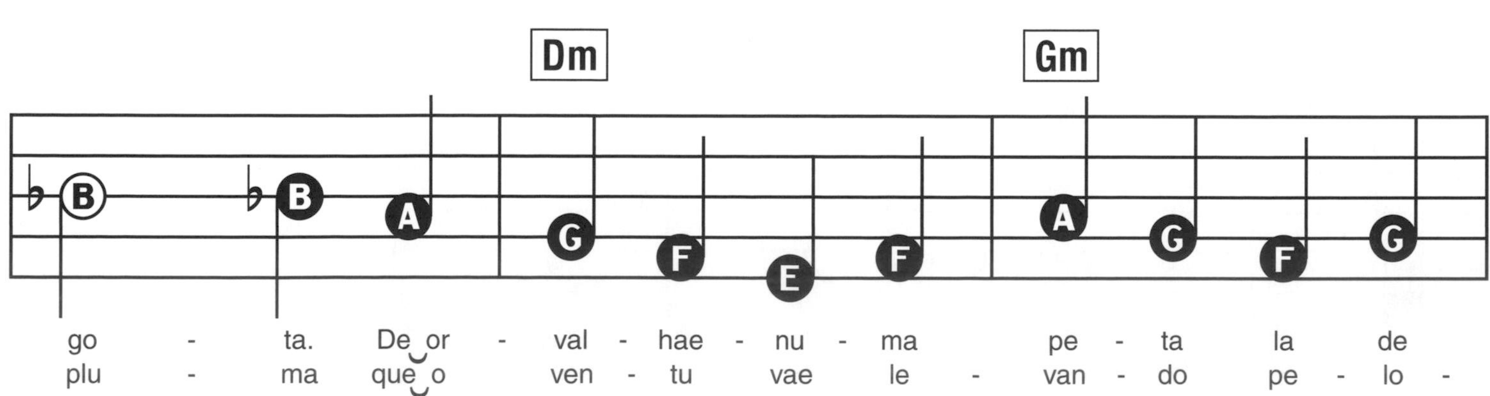

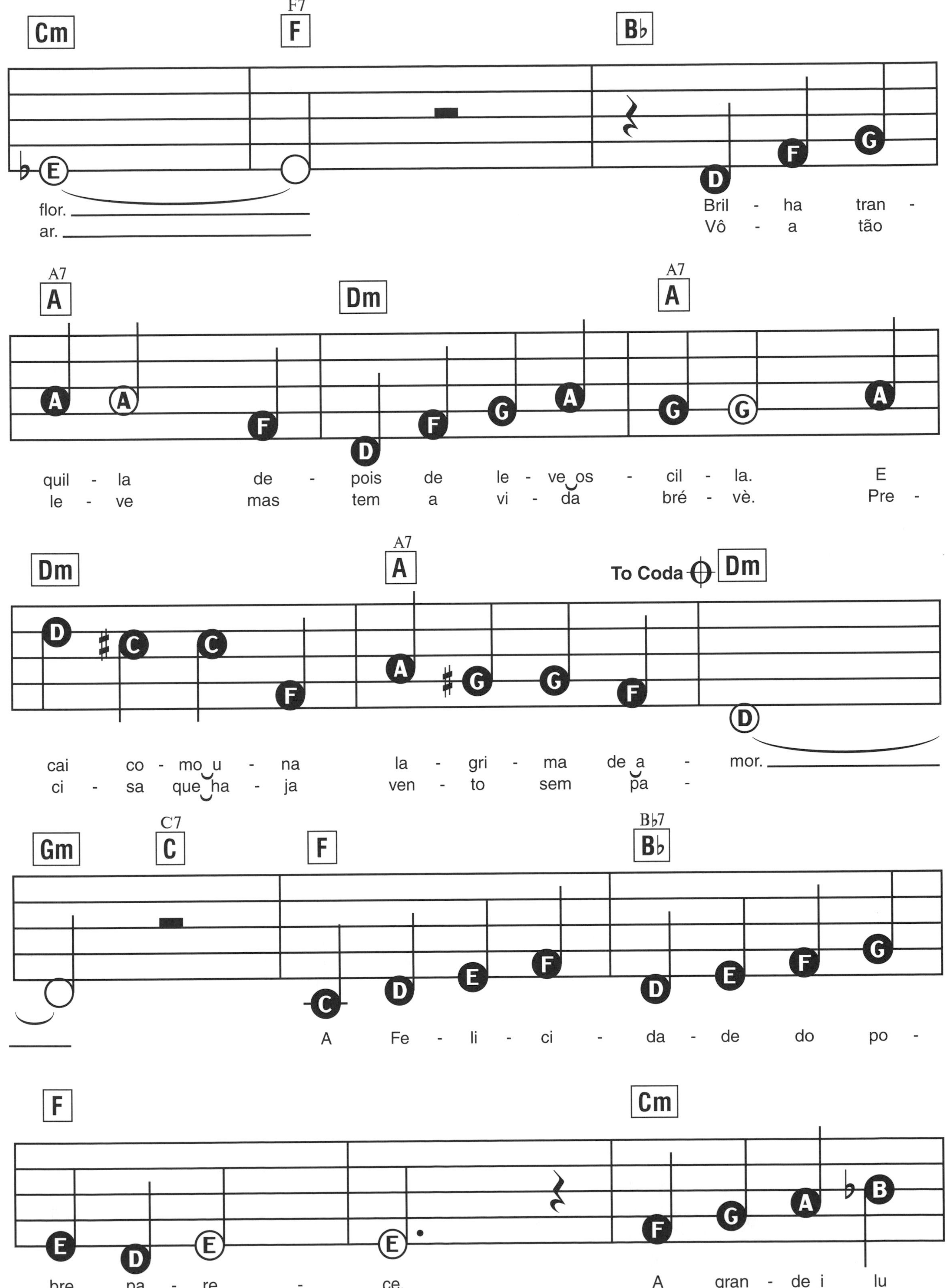
Cm
F7
F
B♭
flor.
ar.
Bril - ha tran -
Vô - a tão
A7
A
Dm
A7
A
quil - la de - pois de le - ve os - cil - la. E
le - ve mas tem a vi - da bré - vè. Pre -
Dm
A7
A
To Coda
Dm
cai co - mo u - na la - gri - ma de a - mor.
ci - sa que ha - ja ven - to sem pa -
Gm
C7
C
F
B♭7
B♭
A Fe - li - ci - da - de do po -
F
Cm
bre pa - re - ce. A gran - de i lu

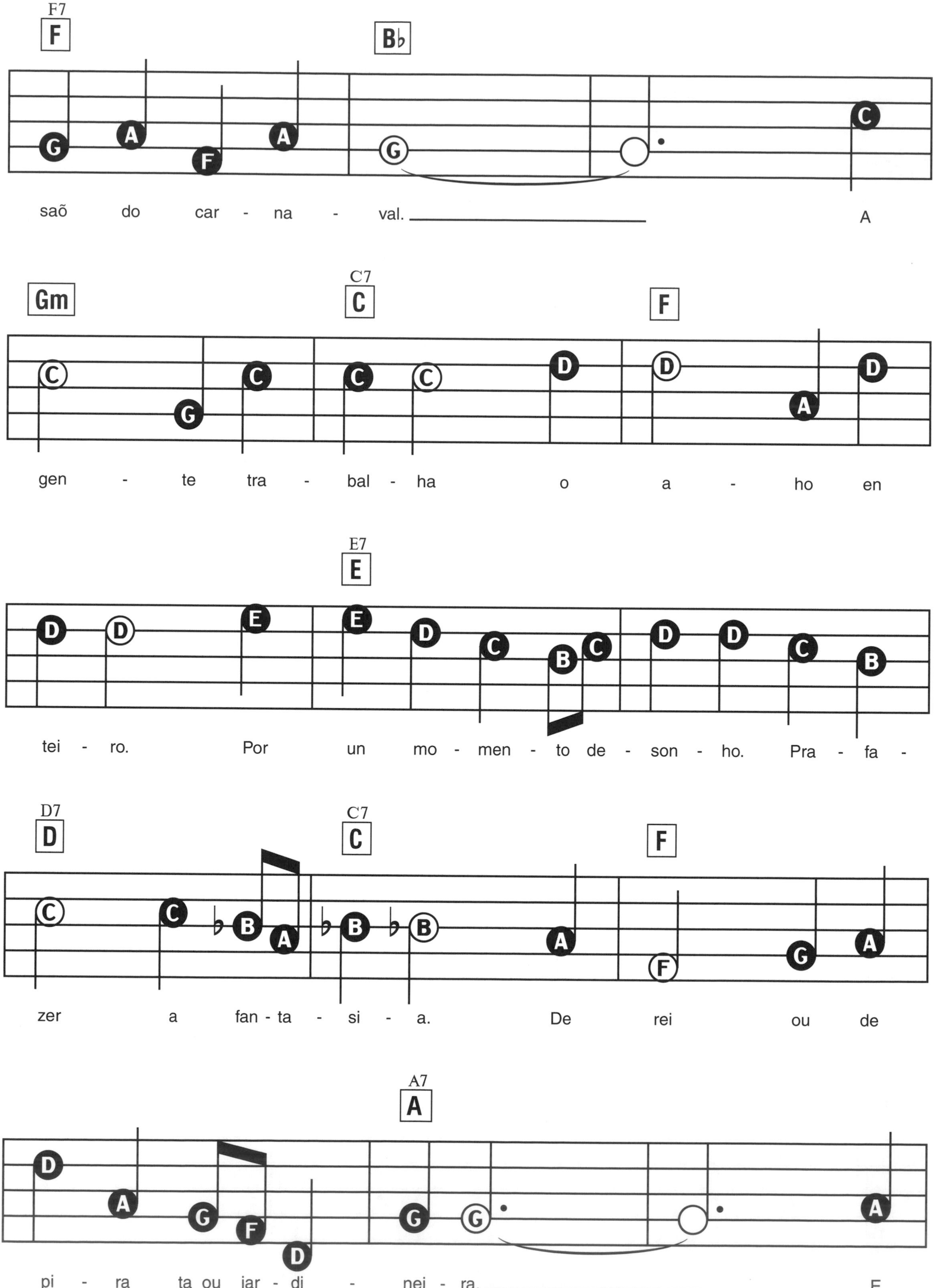
F7 F
B♭
são do car - na - val.
A
Gm
C7 C
F
gen - te tra - bal - ha o a - ho en
E7 E
tei - ro. Por un mo - men - to de - son - ho. Pra - fa -
D7 D
C7 C
F
zer a fan - ta - si - a. De rei ou de
A7 A
pi - ra ta ou jar - di - nei - ra.
E

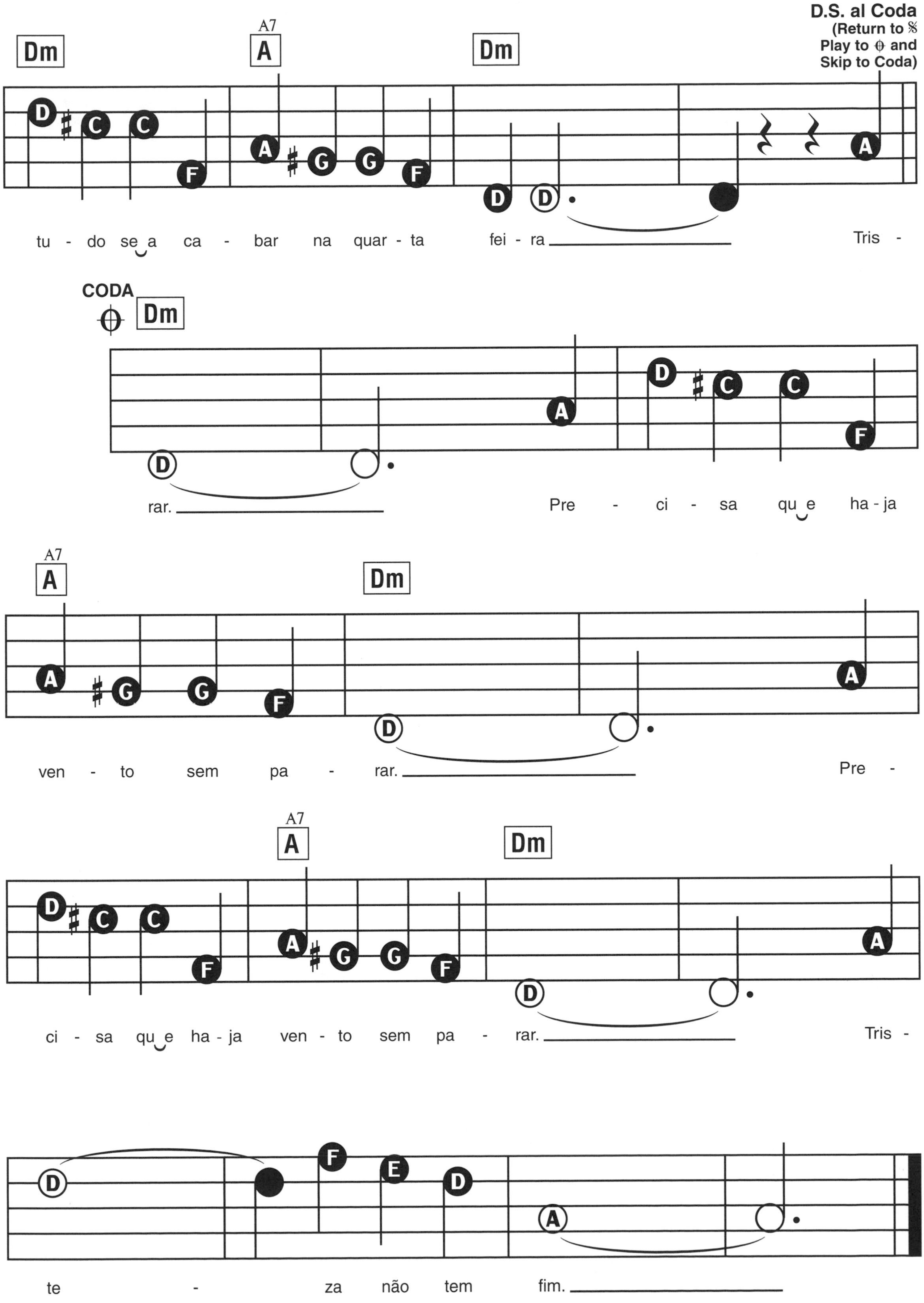

Dm A7 A Dm

D.S. al Coda
(Return to 𝄋 Play to 𝄌 and Skip to Coda)

tu - do se‿a ca - bar na quar - ta fei - ra ____ Tris -

CODA 𝄌 Dm

rar. ____ Pre - ci - sa qu‿e ha - ja

A7 A Dm

ven - to sem pa - rar. ____ Pre -

A7 A Dm

ci - sa qu‿e ha - ja ven - to sem pa - rar. ____ Tris -

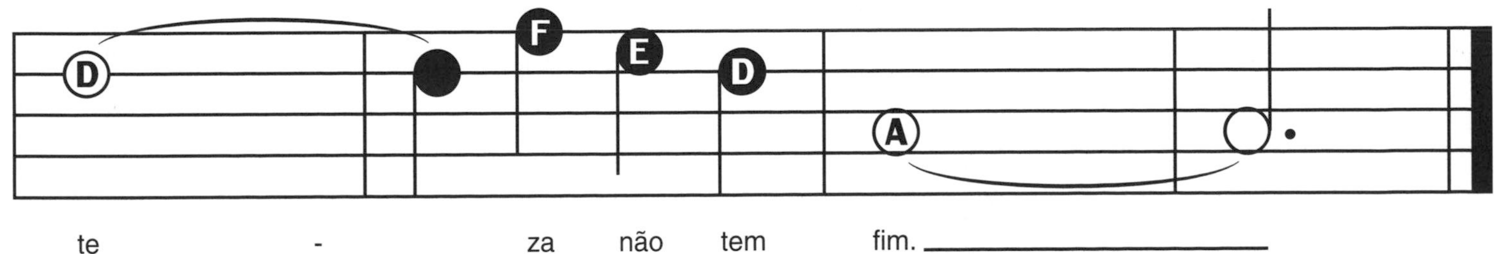

The Girl from Ipanema

(Garôta de Ipanema)

Registration 4
Rhythm: Latin or Bossa Nova

Music by Antonio Carlos Jobim
English Words by Norman Gimbel
Original Words by Vinicius de Moraes

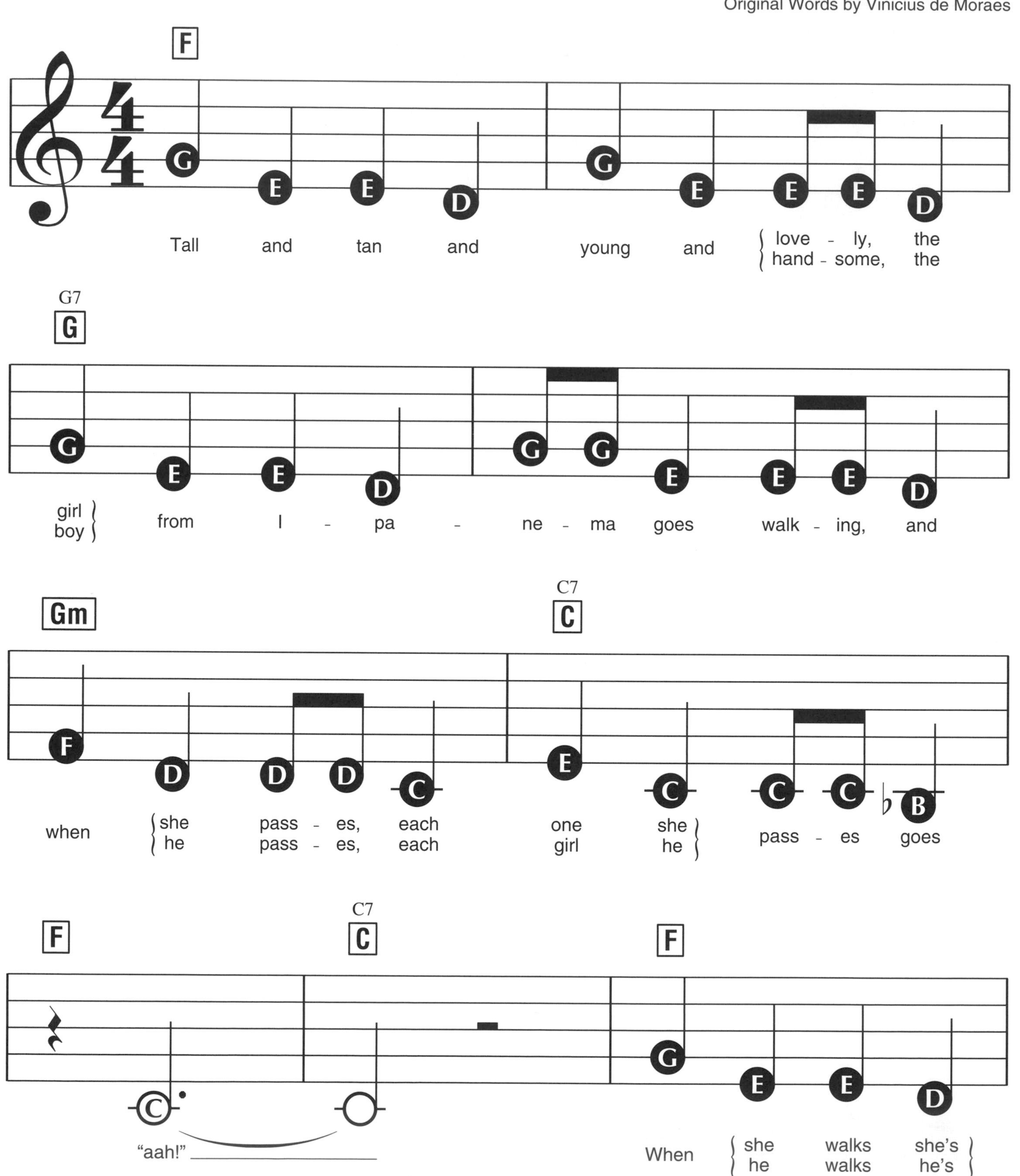

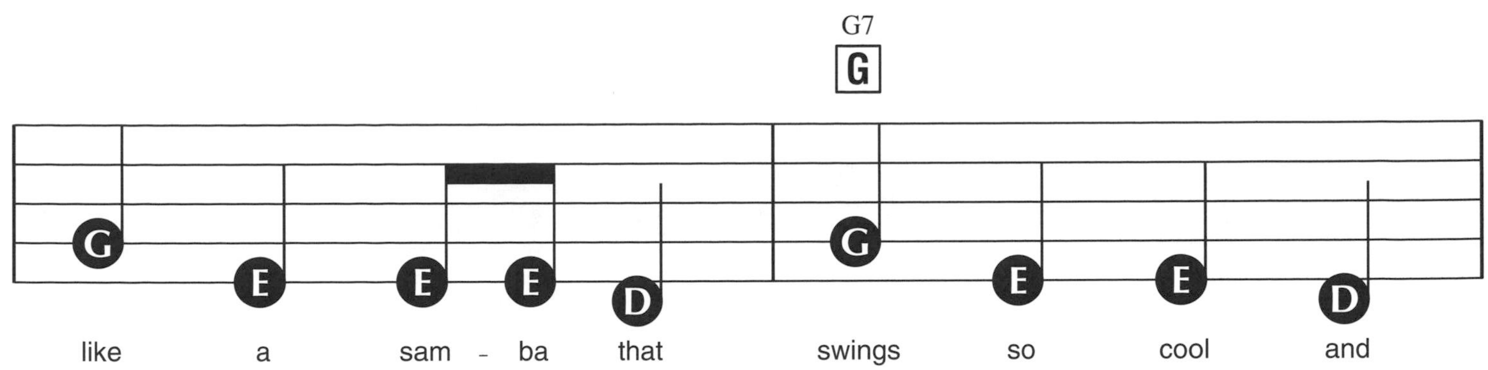
G7
G
G
E
E
E
D
G
E
E
D
like a sam - ba that swings so cool and

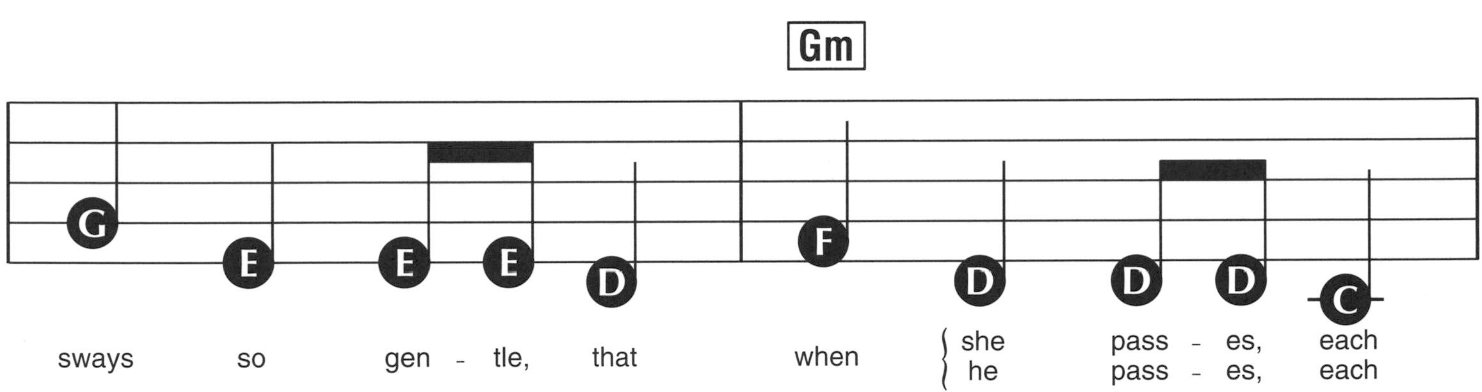
Gm
G
E
E
E
D
F
D
D
D
C
sways so gen - tle, that when she pass - es, each
he pass - es, each

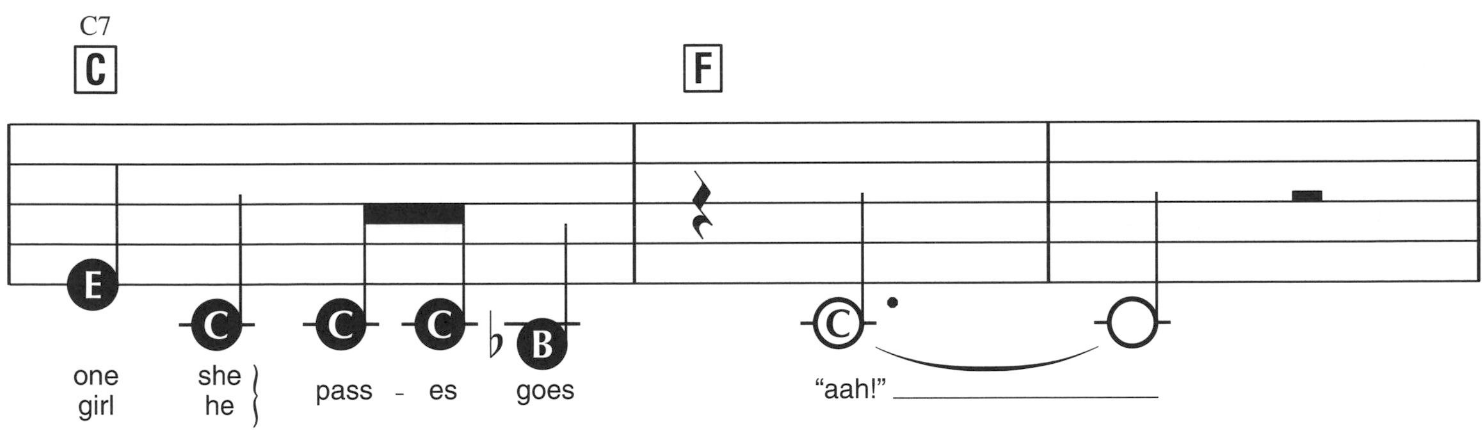
C7
C
F
E
C
C
C
B
C
one she pass - es goes "aah!"
girl he

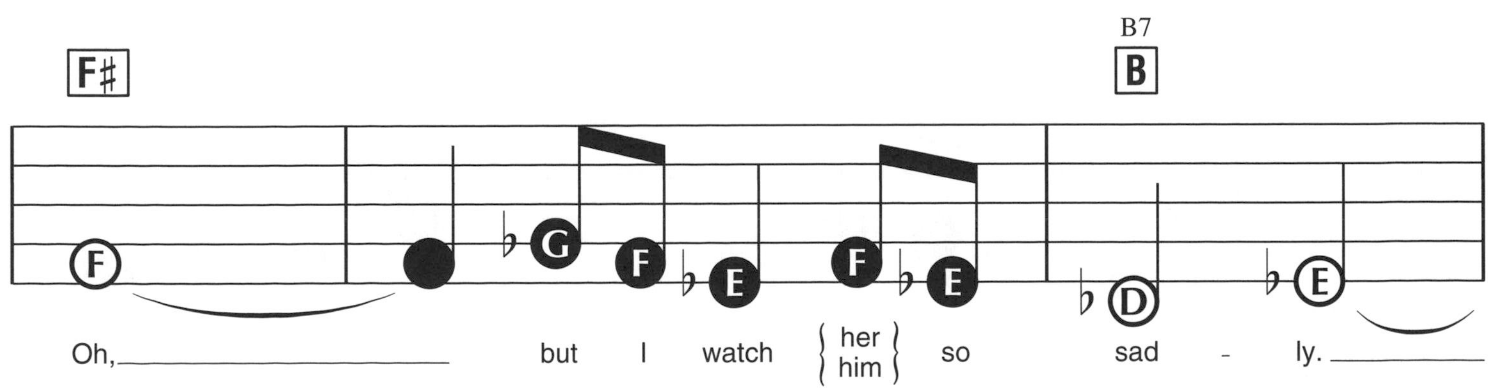
F♯
B7
B
F
G
F
E
F
E
D
E
Oh, but I watch her so sad - ly.
him

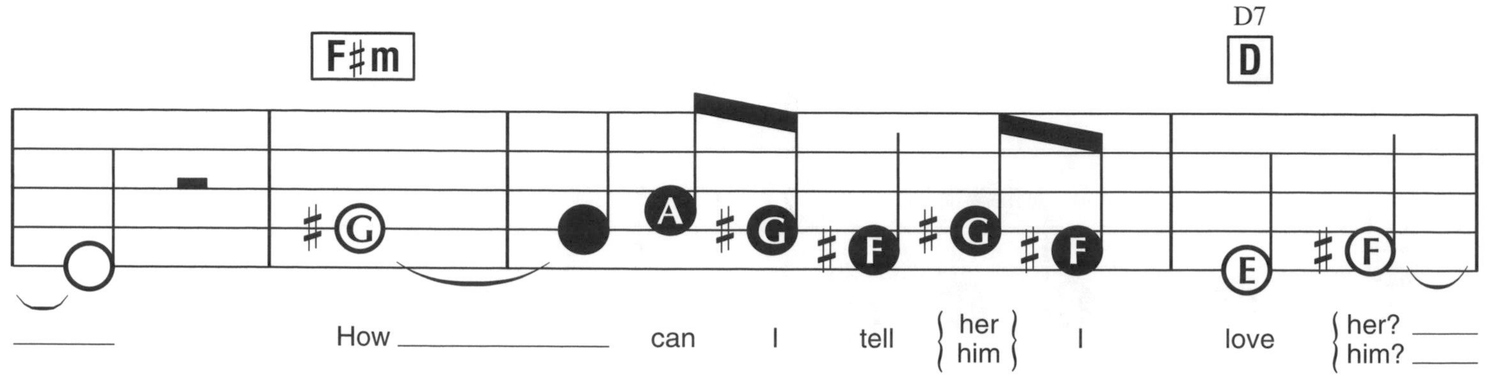
F♯m
D7
D
How can I tell her / him I love her? / him?

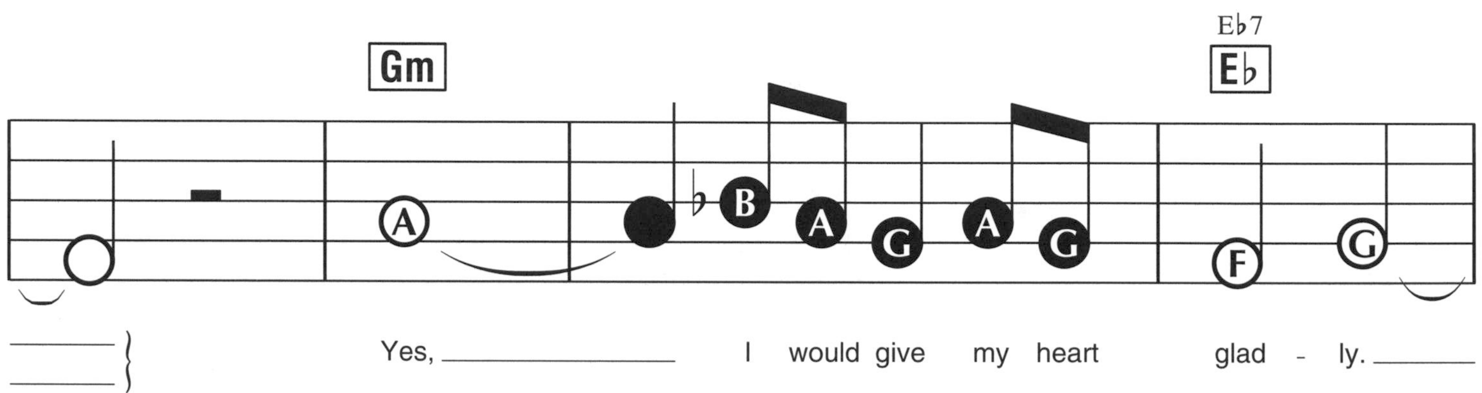
Gm
E♭7
E♭
Yes, I would give my heart glad - ly.

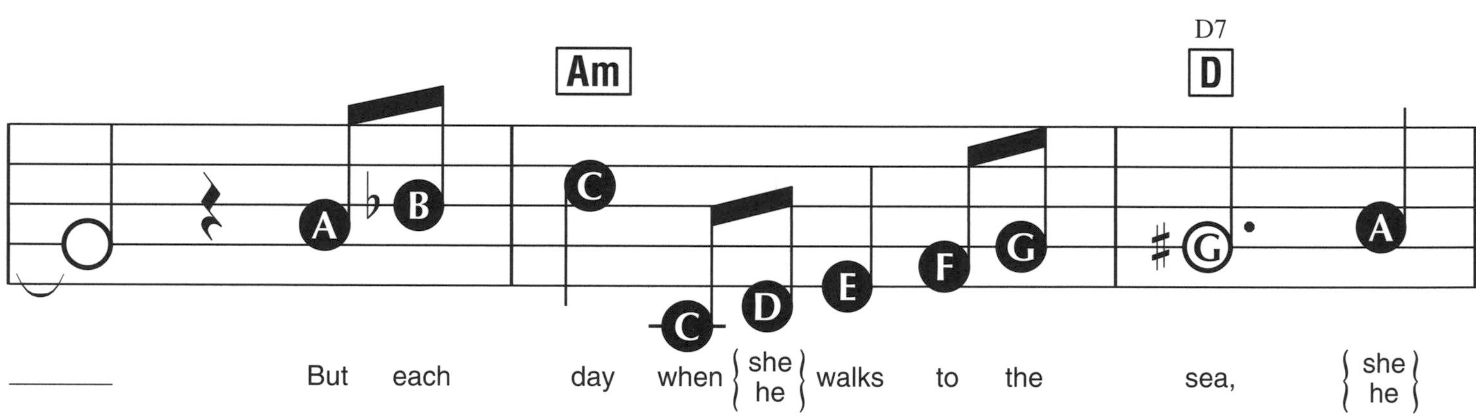
Am
D7
D
But each day when she / he walks to the sea, she / he

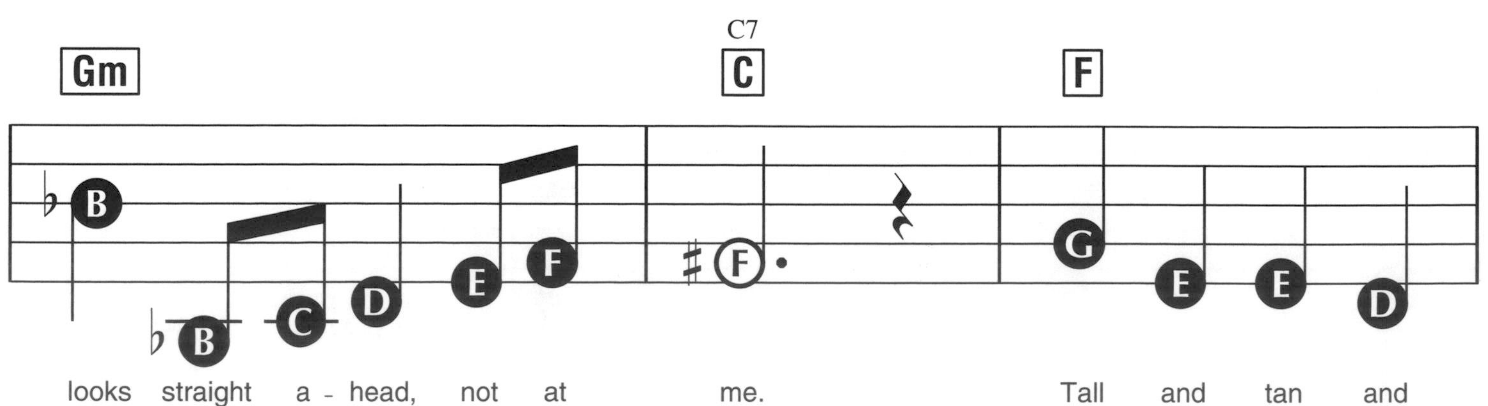
Gm
C7
C
F
looks straight a - head, not at me. Tall and tan and

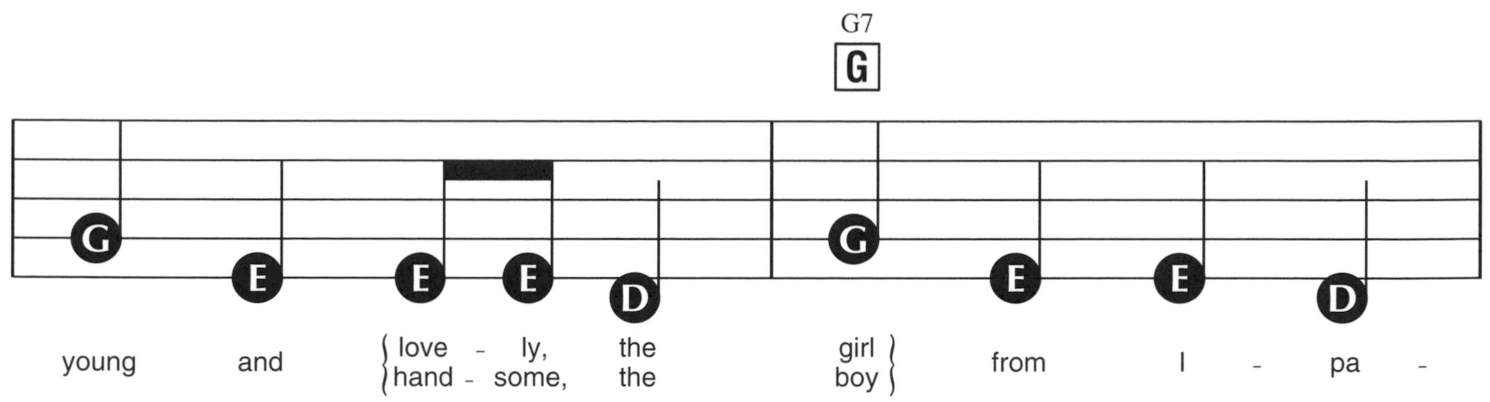

G7
G
G E E E D G E E D
young and love - ly, the girl from I - pa -
hand - some, the boy

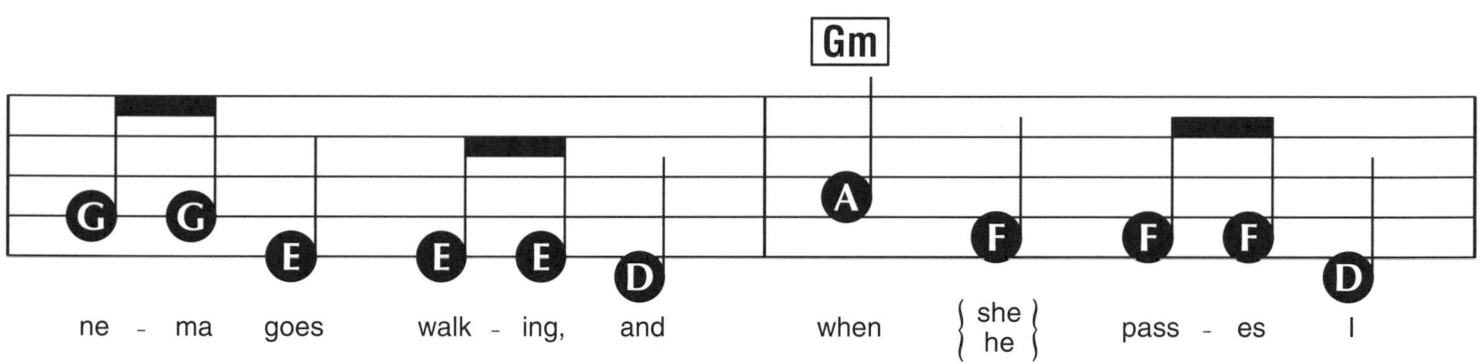

Gm
G G E E E D A F F F D
ne - ma goes walk - ing, and when she pass - es I
he

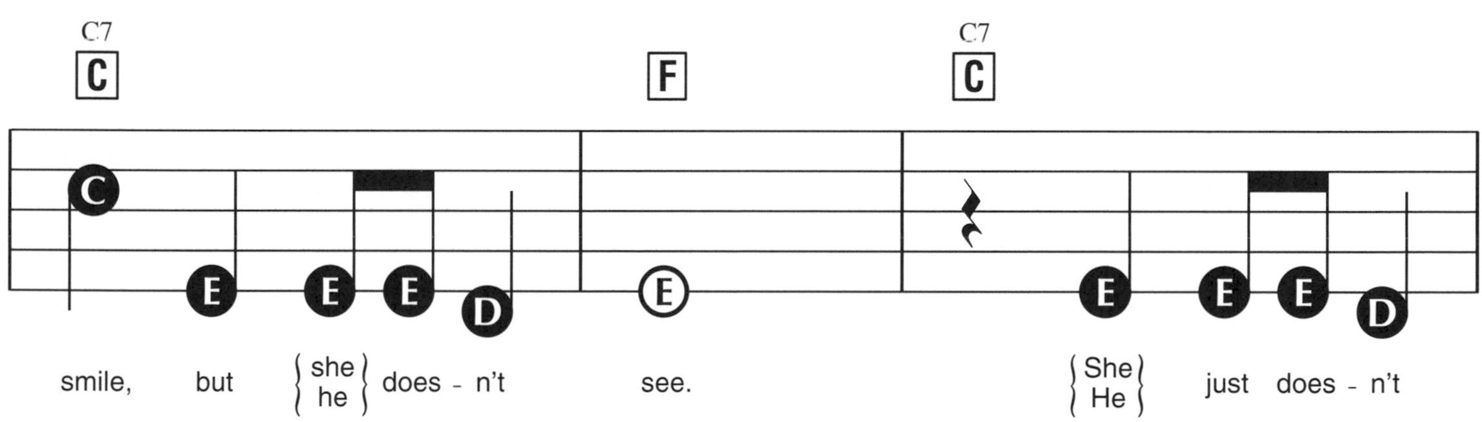

C7
C
F
C7
C
C E E E D E E E E D
smile, but she does - n't see. She just does - n't
he He

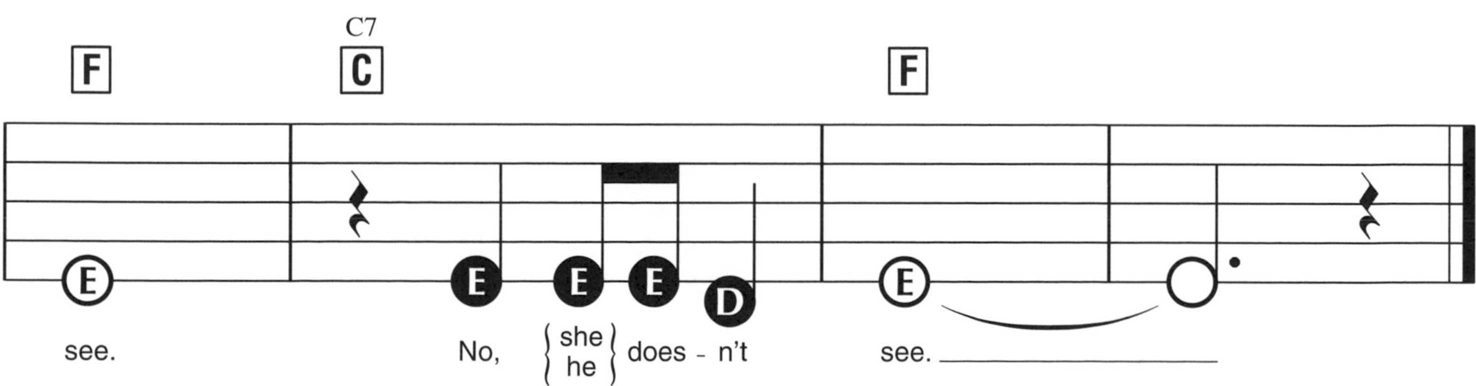

F
C7
C
F
E E E E D E
see. No, she does - n't see.
he

How Insensitive
(Insensatez)

Registration 8
Rhythm: Bossa Nova or Latin

Music by Antonio Carlos Jobim
Original Words by Vinicius de Moraes
English Words by Norman Gimbel

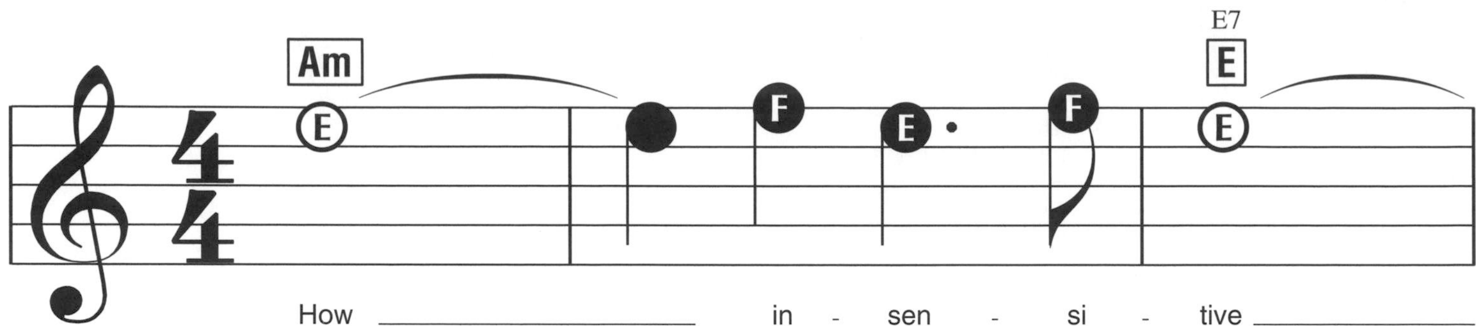

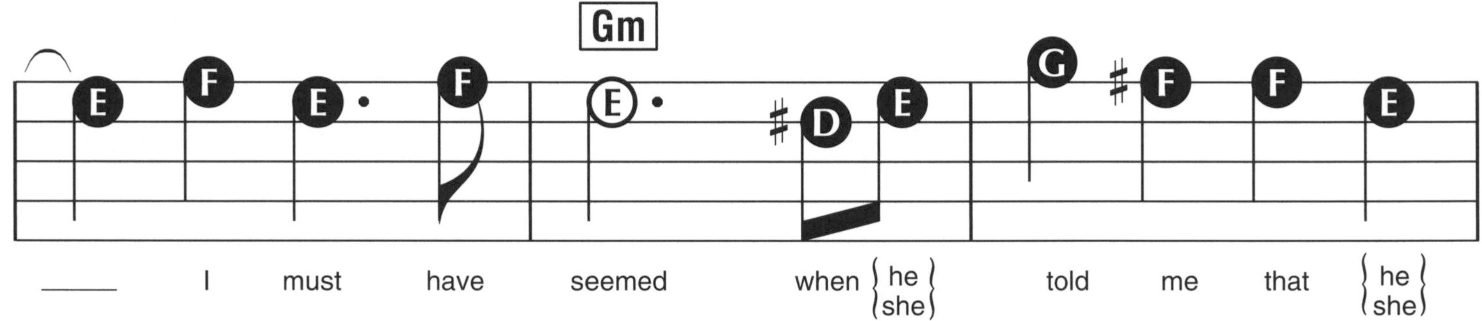

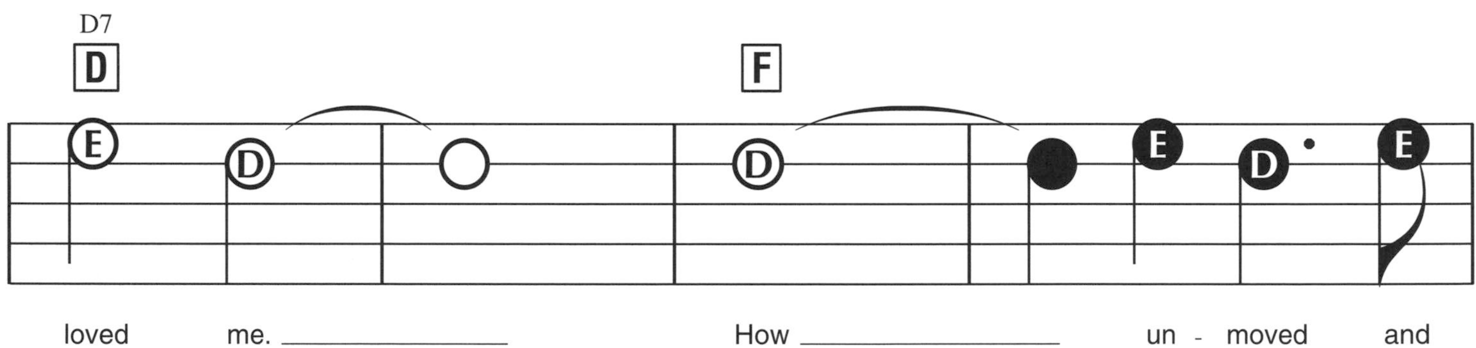

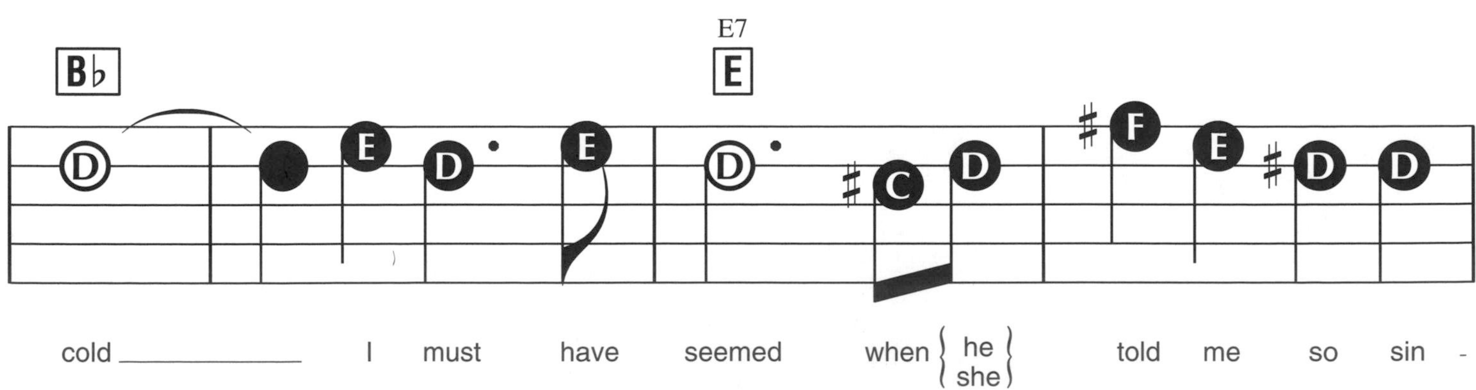

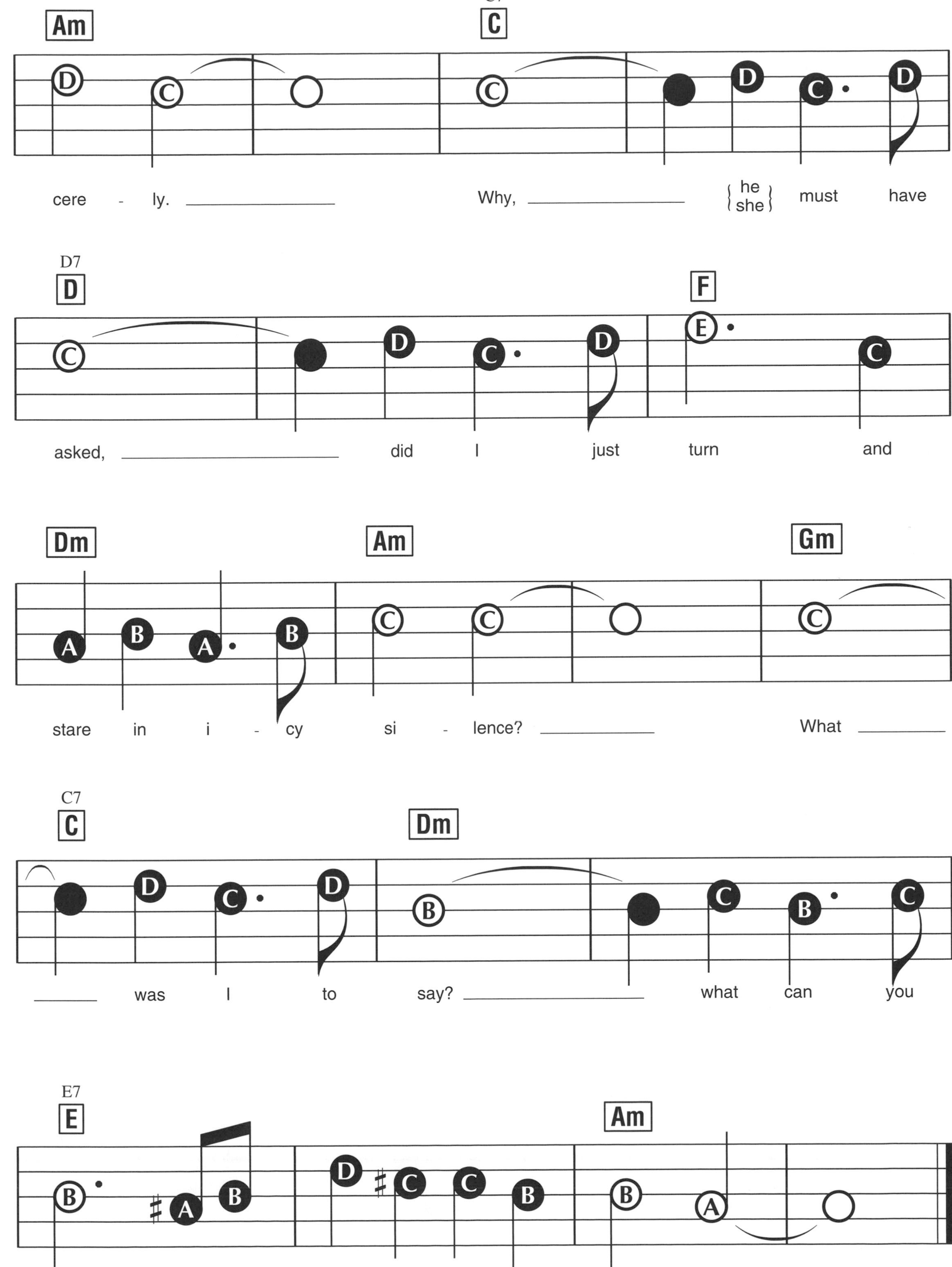
Am
C7
C
cere - ly.
Why,
he
she
must have
D7
D
F
asked,
did I just turn and
Dm
Am
Gm
stare in i - cy si - lence?
What
C7
C
Dm
was I to say?
what can you
E7
E
Am
say when a love af - fair is o - ver?

Meditation
(Meditacão)

Registration 5
Rhythm: Rhumba or Latin

Music by Antonio Carlos Jobim
Original Words by Newton Mendonca
English Words by Norman Gimbel

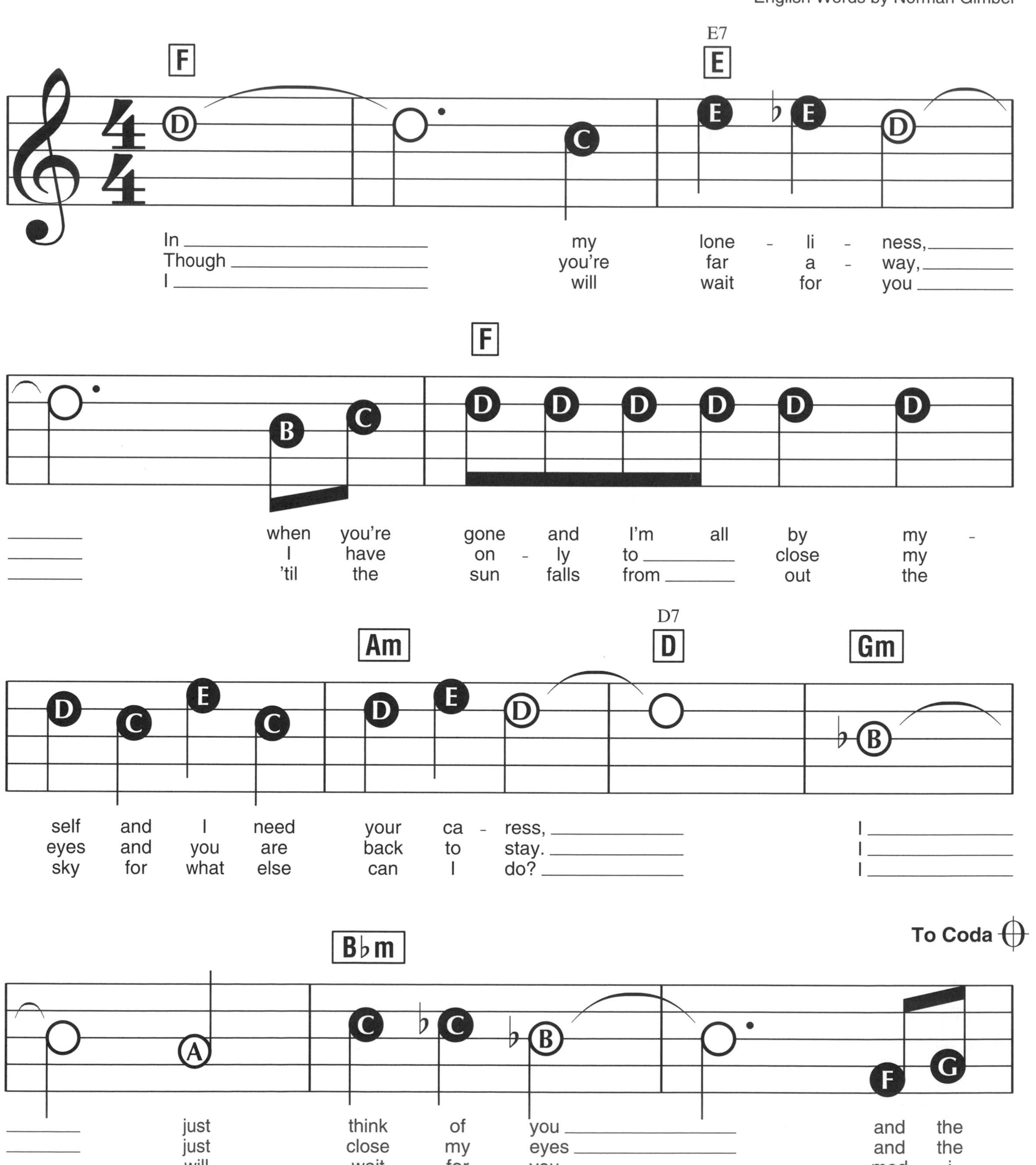

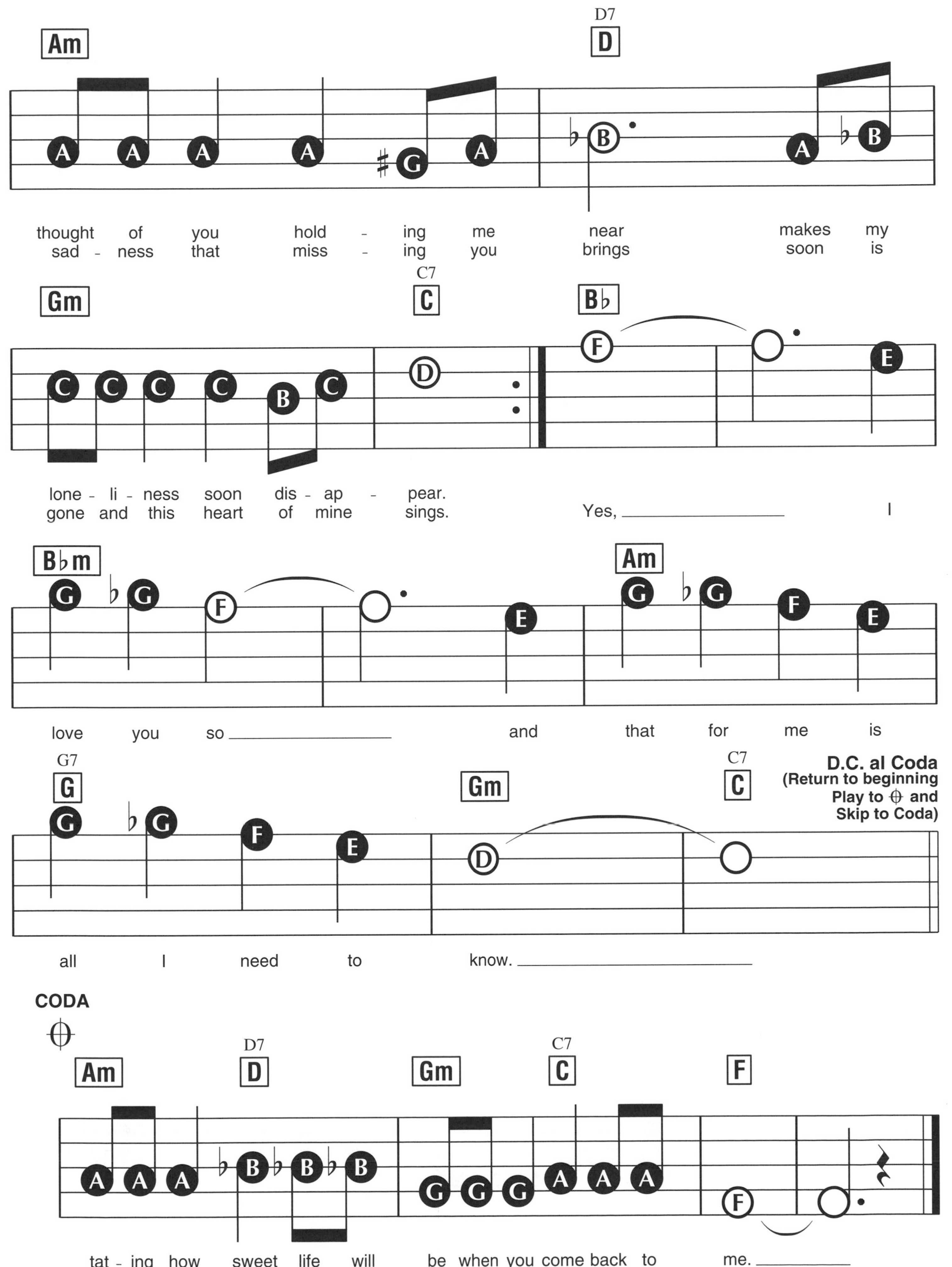
Am
D7
D
thought of you hold - ing me near makes my
sad - ness that miss - ing you brings soon is
Gm
C7
C
B♭
lone - li - ness soon dis - ap - pear.
gone and this heart of mine sings.
Yes, I
B♭m
Am
love you so and that for me is
G7
G
Gm
C7
C
D.C. al Coda
(Return to beginning
Play to ⊕ and
Skip to Coda)
all I need to know.
CODA
Am
D7
D
Gm
C7
C
F
tat - ing how sweet life will be when you come back to me.

O Grande Amor

Registration 4
Rhythm: Bossa Nova or Latin

Words and Music by Antonio Carlos Jobim
and Vinicius de Moraes

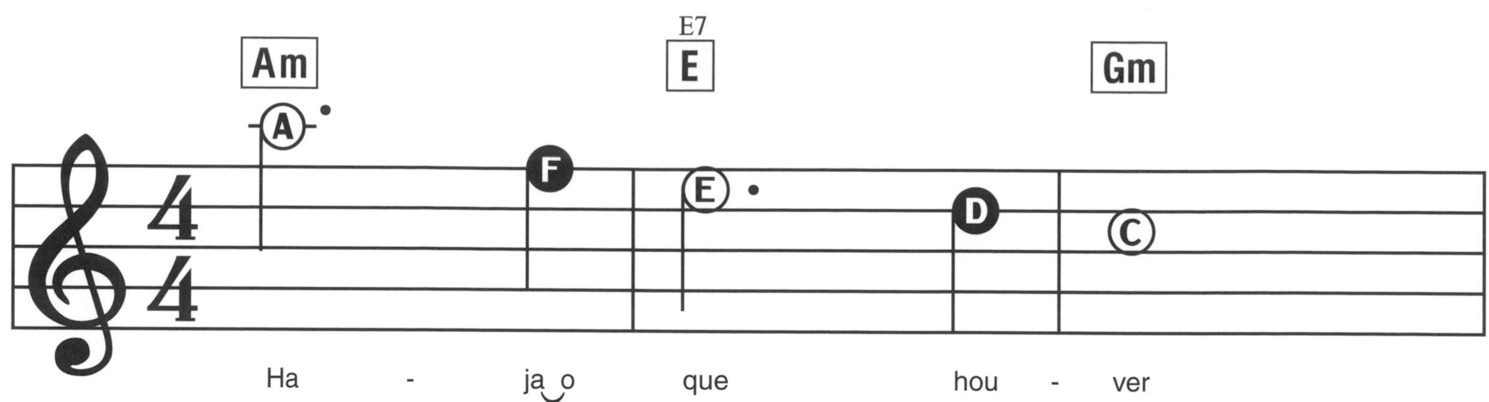

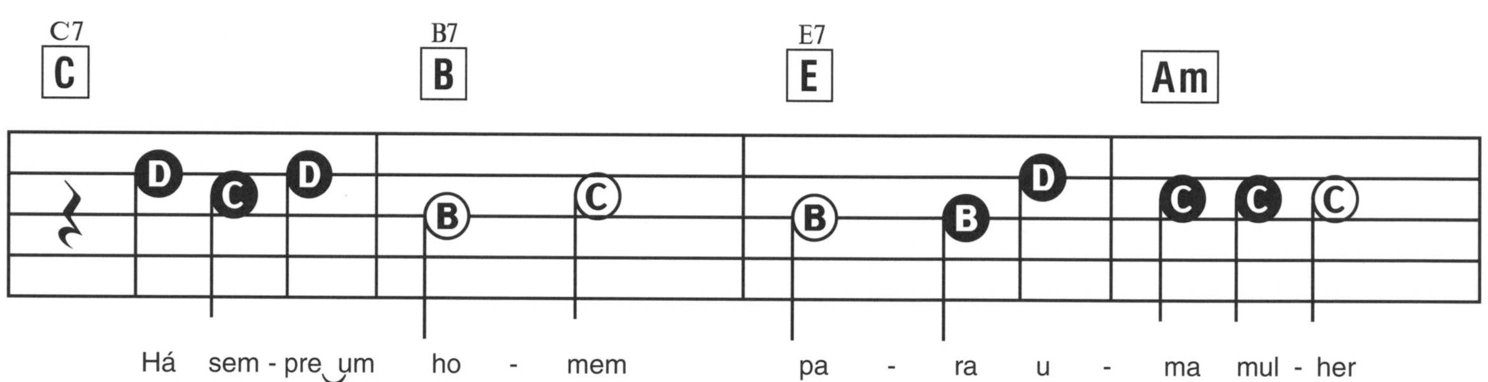

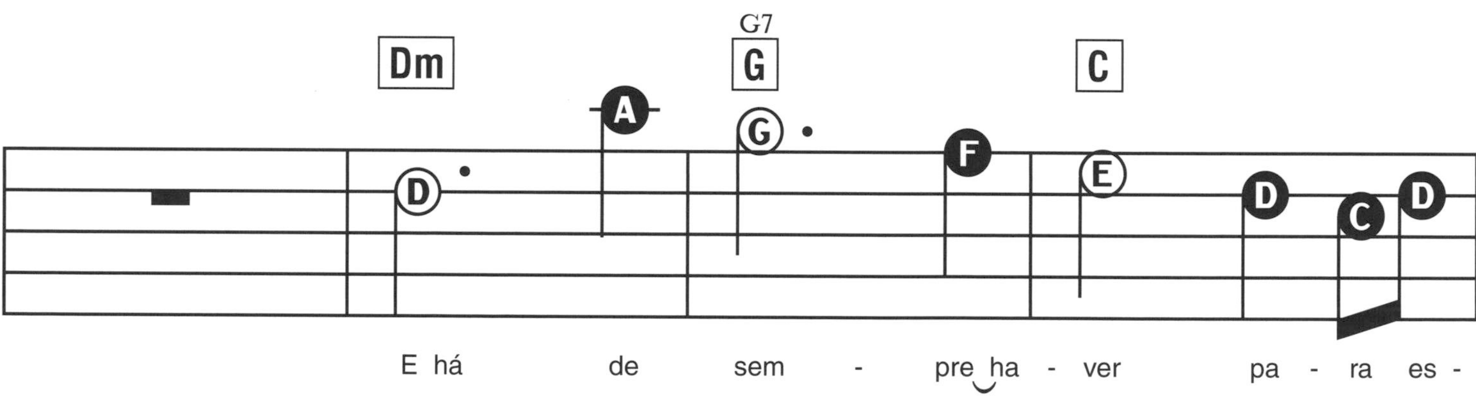

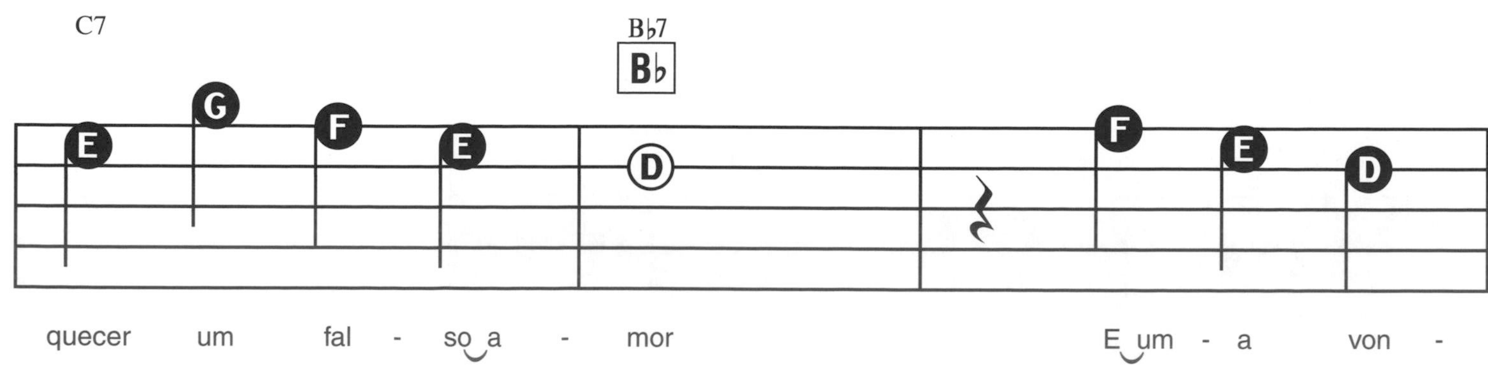

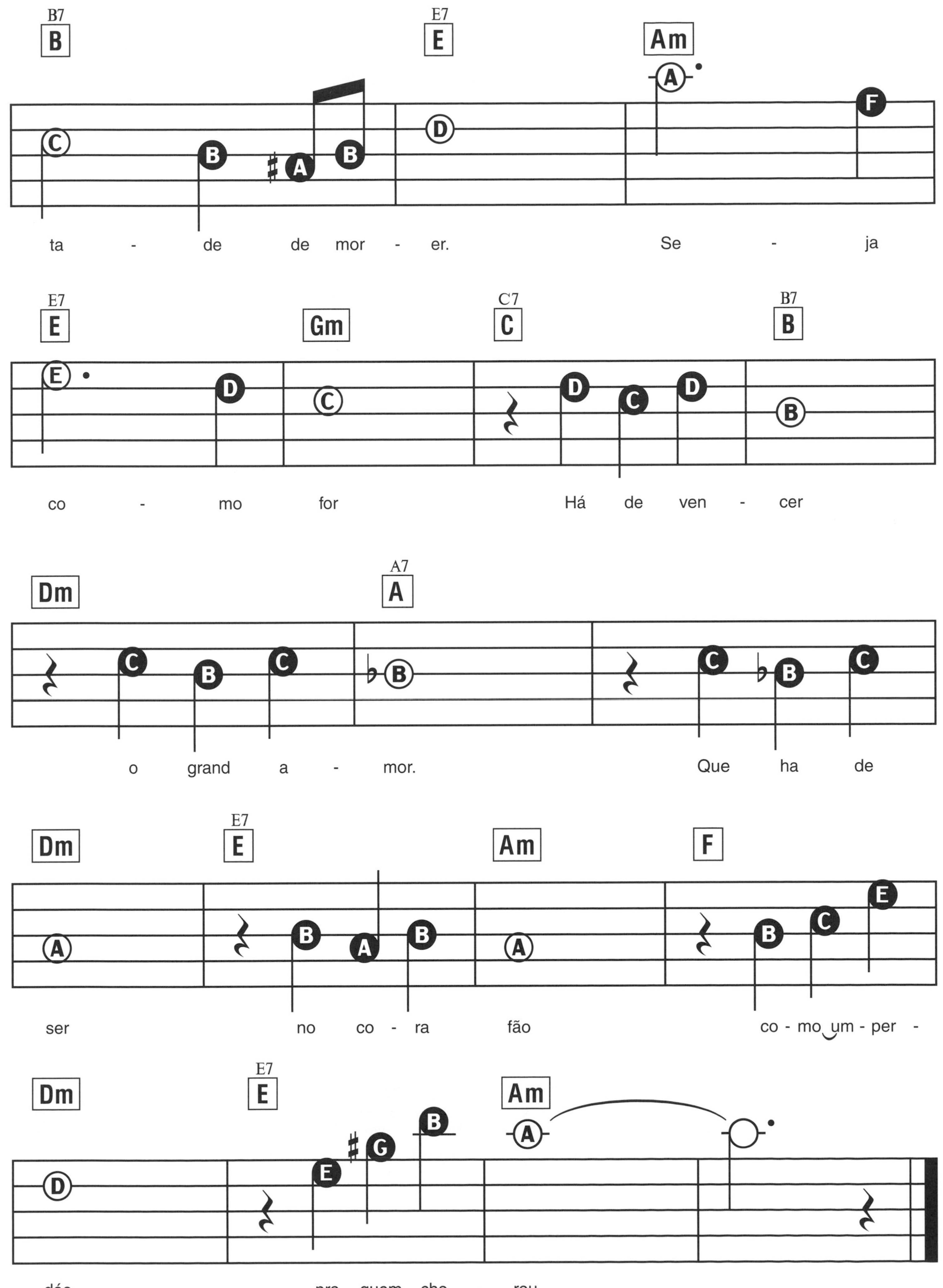
B7
B
E7
E
Am
ta - de de mor - er.
Se - ja
E7
E
Gm
C7
C
B7
B
co - mo for
Há de ven - cer
Dm
A7
A
o grand a - mor.
Que ha de
Dm
E7
E
Am
F
ser no co - ra fão co - mo um - per -
Dm
E7
E
Am
dáo pra quem cho - rou.

Once I Loved
(Amor em Paz)
(Love in Peace)

Registration 8
Rhythm: Bossa Nova or Latin

Music by Antonio Carlos Jobim
Portuguese Lyrics by Vinicius de Moraes
English Lyrics by Ray Gilbert

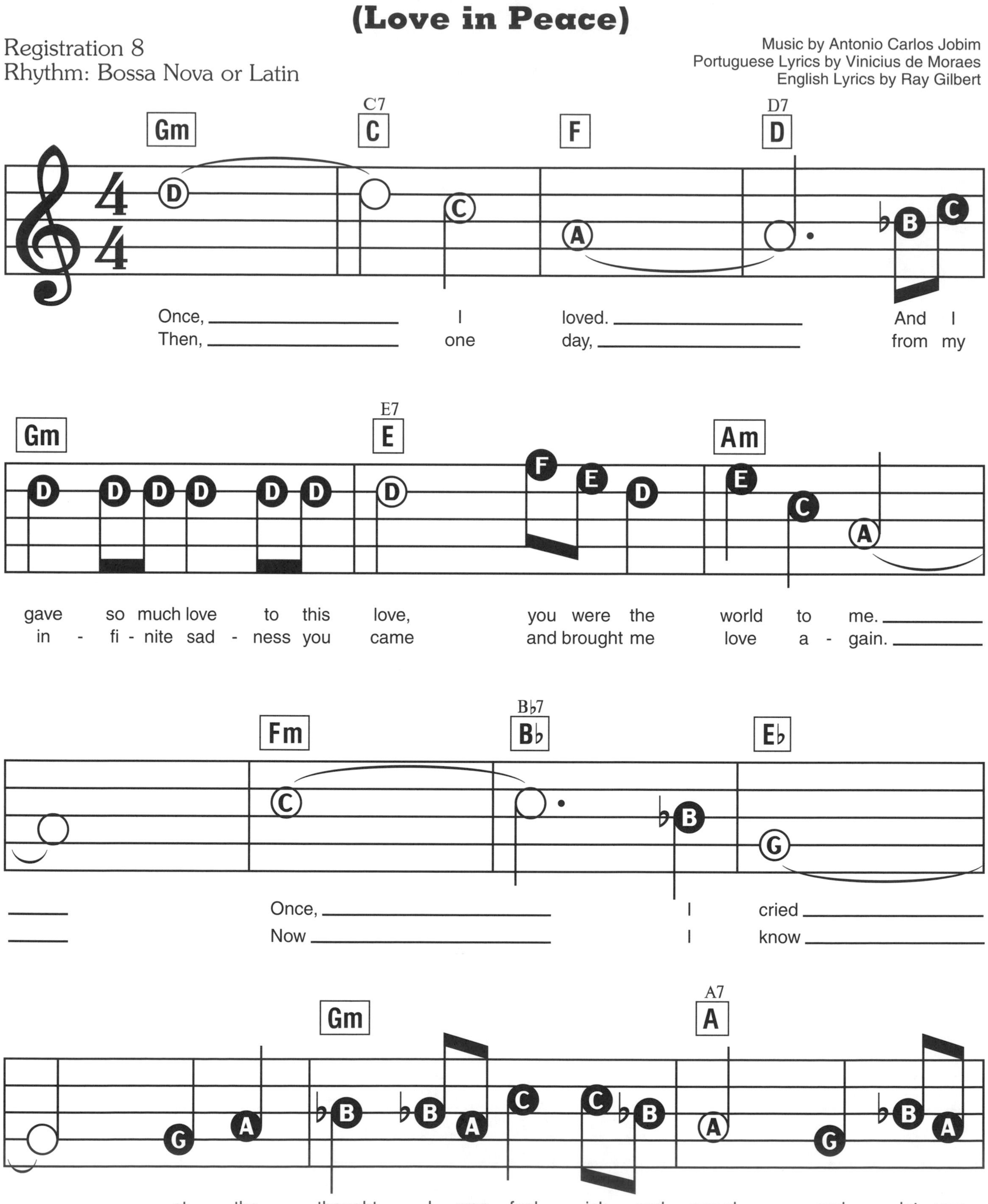

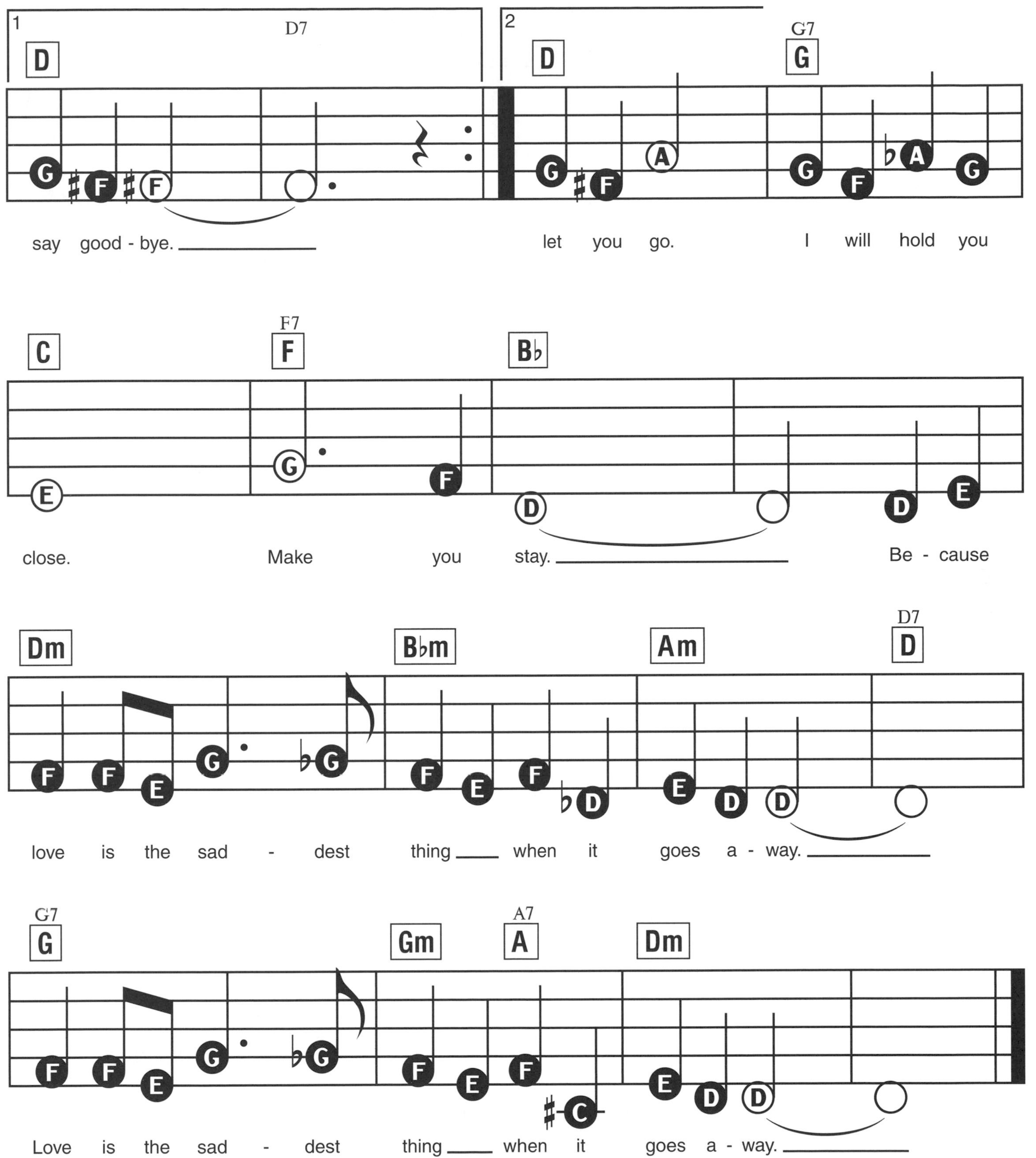

Portuguese Lyrics

Eu amei, e amei ai de mim muito mais do que devia amar.
E chorei ao sentir que eu iria sofrer e me deseperar.

Foi antão, que da minha infinita triztesa aconteceu você.
Encontrei, em você a razão de viver e de amar em paz
E não sofrer mais. Nunca mais.
Porque o amor é a coisa mais triste quando se desfaz.
O amor é a coisa mais triste quando se desfaz.

One Note Samba
(Samba De Uma Nota So)

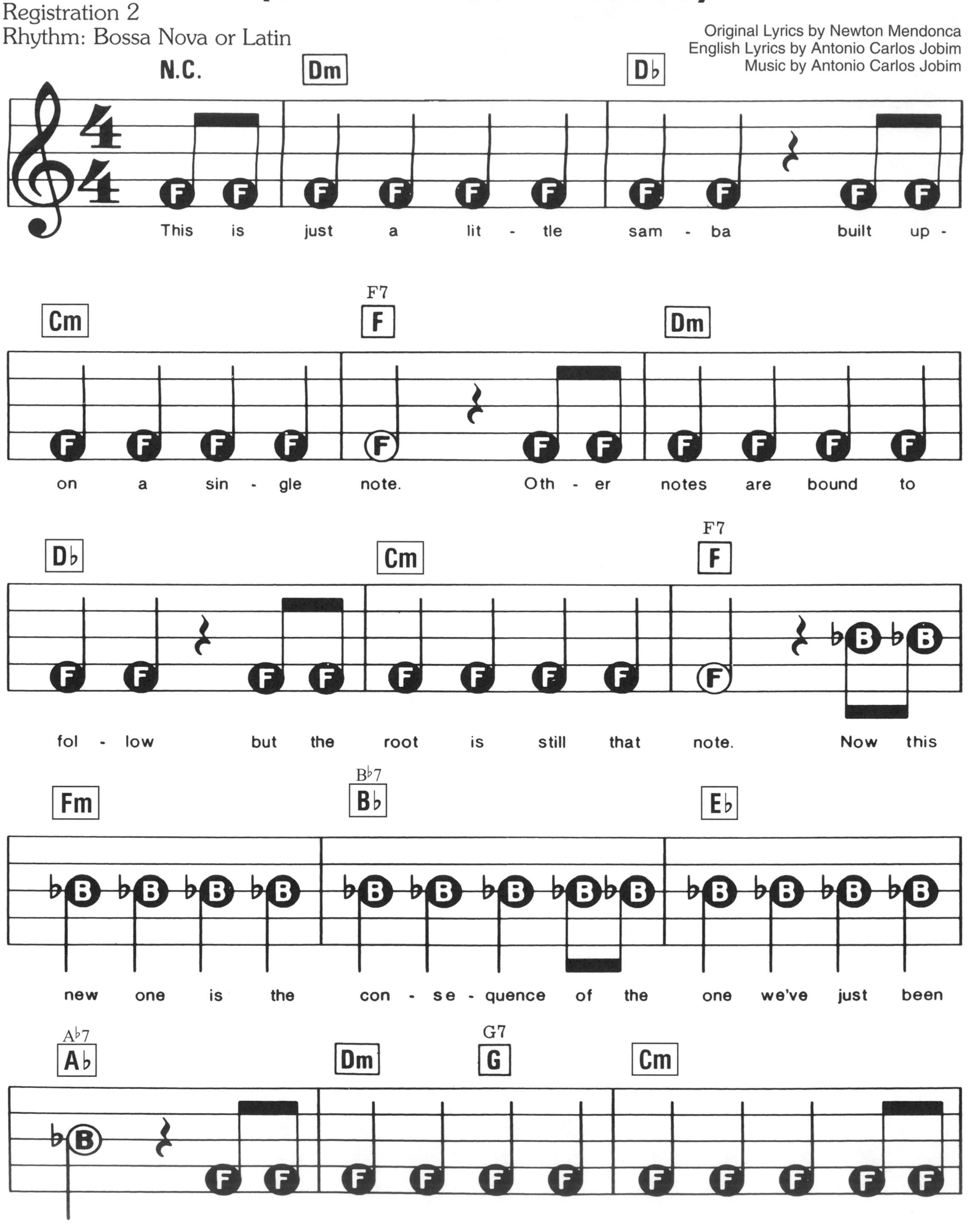

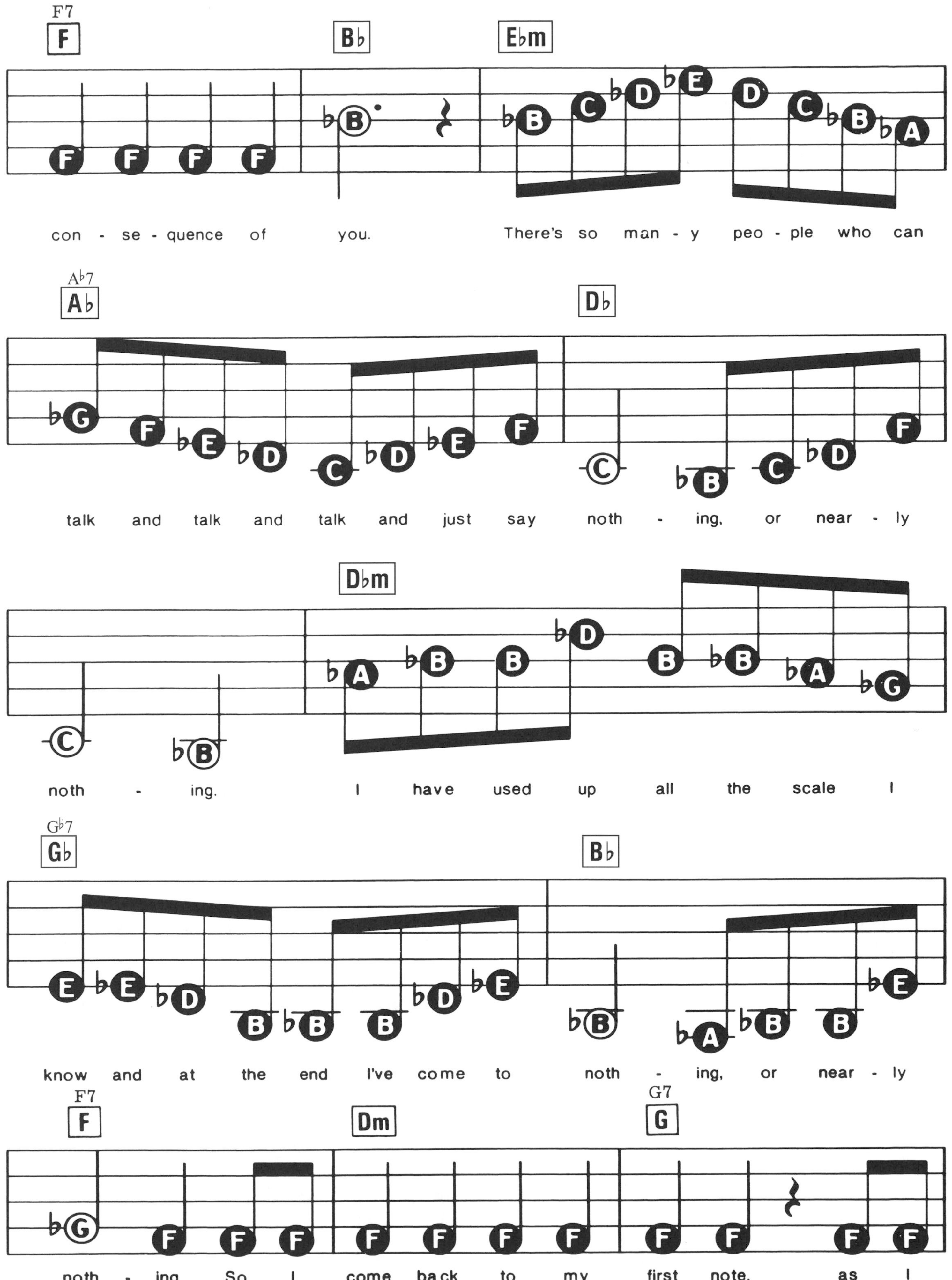
F7
F
B♭
E♭m
con - se - quence of you. There's so man - y peo - ple who can
A♭7
A♭
D♭
talk and talk and talk and just say noth - ing, or near - ly
D♭m
noth - ing. I have used up all the scale I
G♭7
G♭
B♭
know and at the end I've come to noth - ing, or near - ly
F7
F
Dm
G7
G
noth - ing. So I come back to my first note, as I

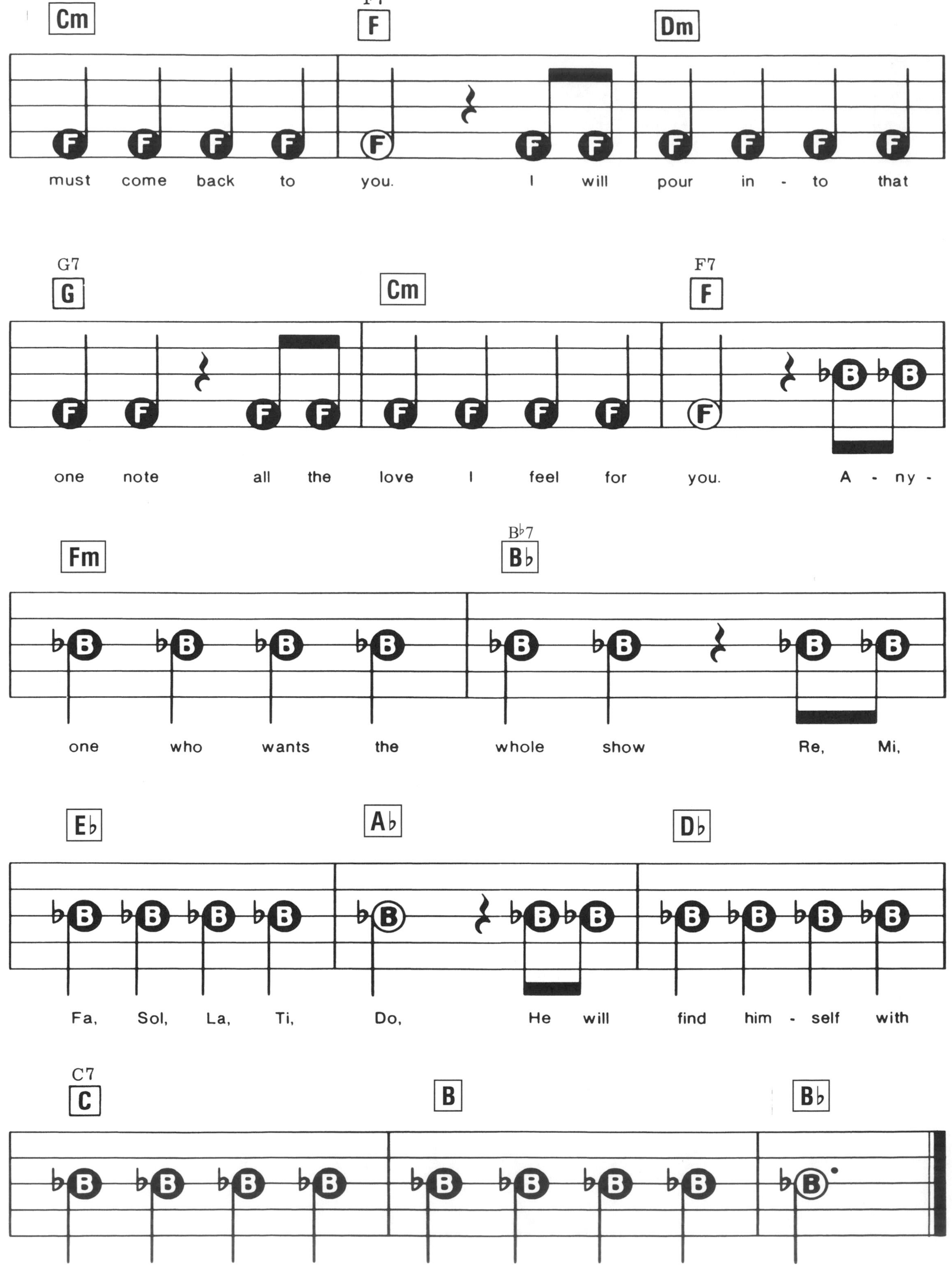
Cm
F7
F
Dm
must come back to you. I will pour in - to that
G7
G
Cm
F7
F
one note all the love I feel for you. A - ny -
Fm
B♭7
B♭
one who wants the whole show Re, Mi,
E♭
A♭
D♭
Fa, Sol, La, Ti, Do, He will find him - self with
C7
C
B
B♭
no show. Bet - ter play the note you know.

Quiet Nights of Quiet Stars
(Corcovado)

Registration 4
Rhythm: Bossa Nova or Latin

English Words by Gene Lees
Original Words and Music by Antonio Carlos Jobim

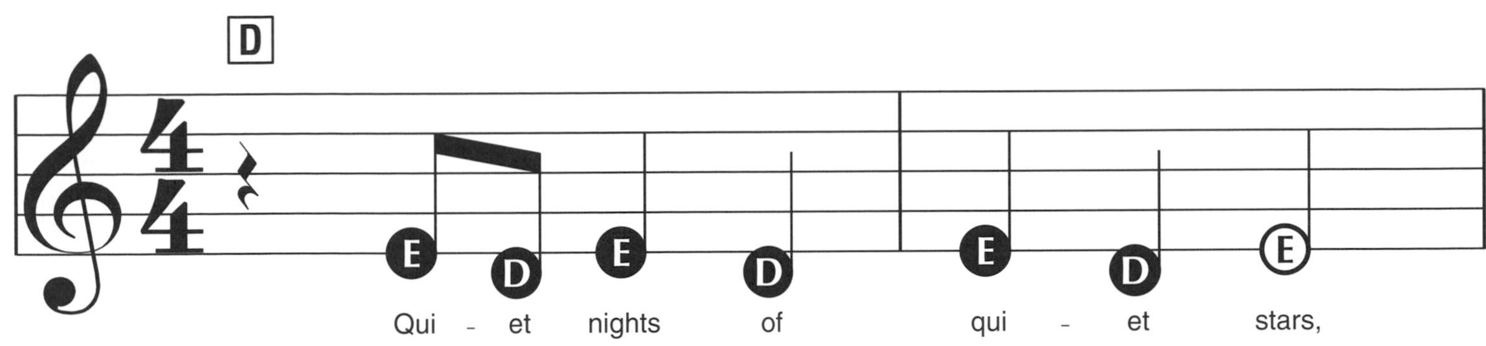

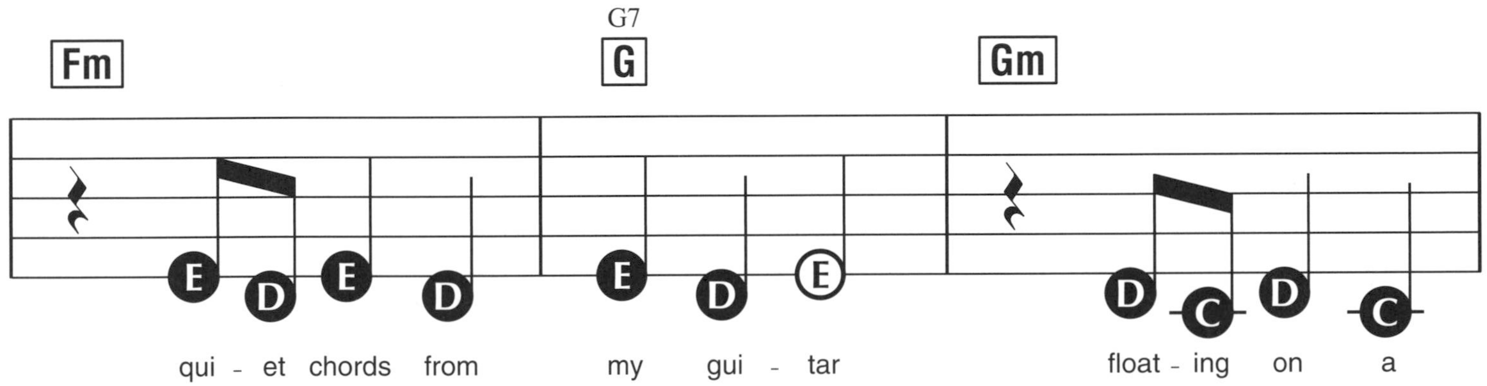

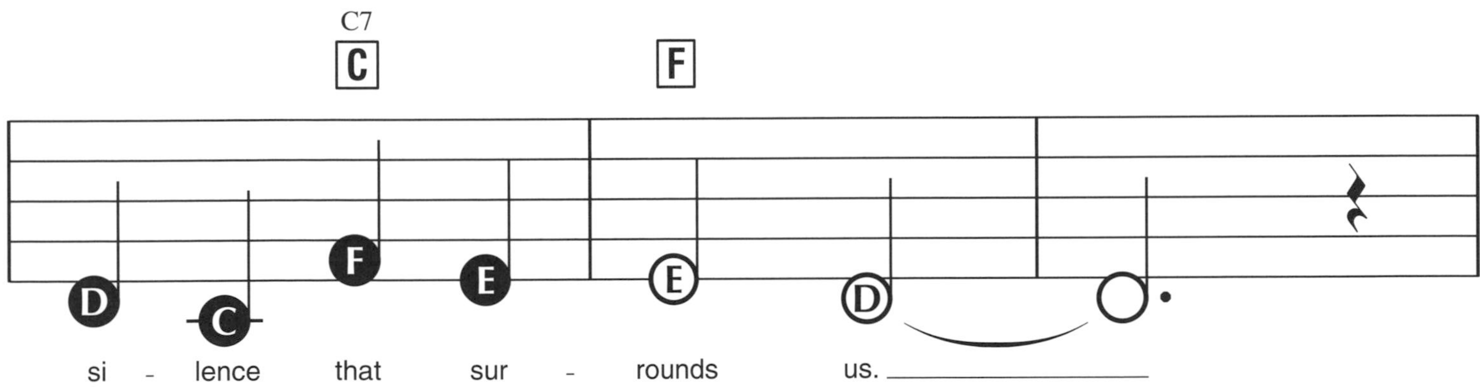

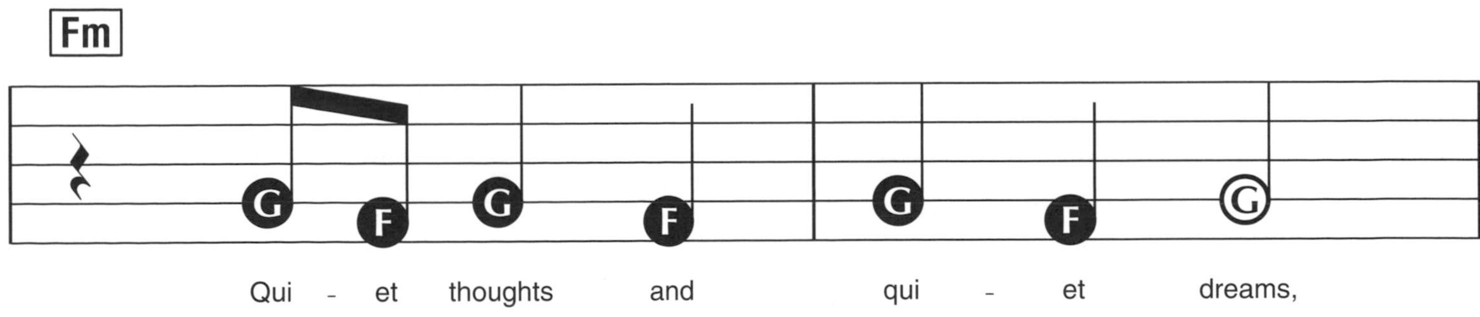

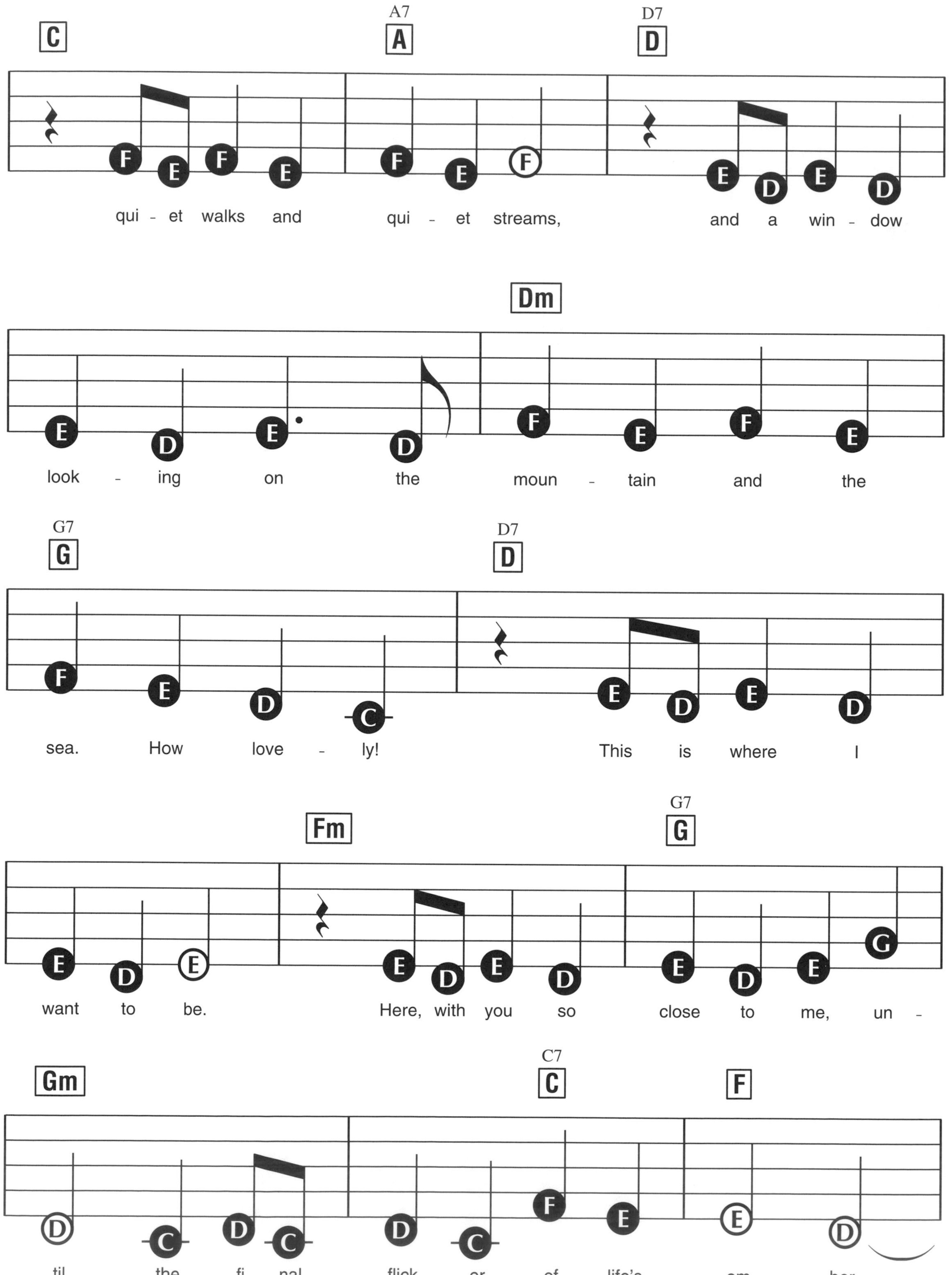
C
A7
A
D7
D
F E F E F E F E D E D
qui - et walks and qui - et streams, and a win - dow
Dm
E D E D F E F E
look - ing on the moun - tain and the
G7
G
D7
D
F E D C E D E D
sea. How love - ly! This is where I
Fm
G7
G
E D E E D E D E D E G
want to be. Here, with you so close to me, un -
Gm
C7
C
F
D C D C D C F E E D
til the fi - nal flick - er of life's em - ber.

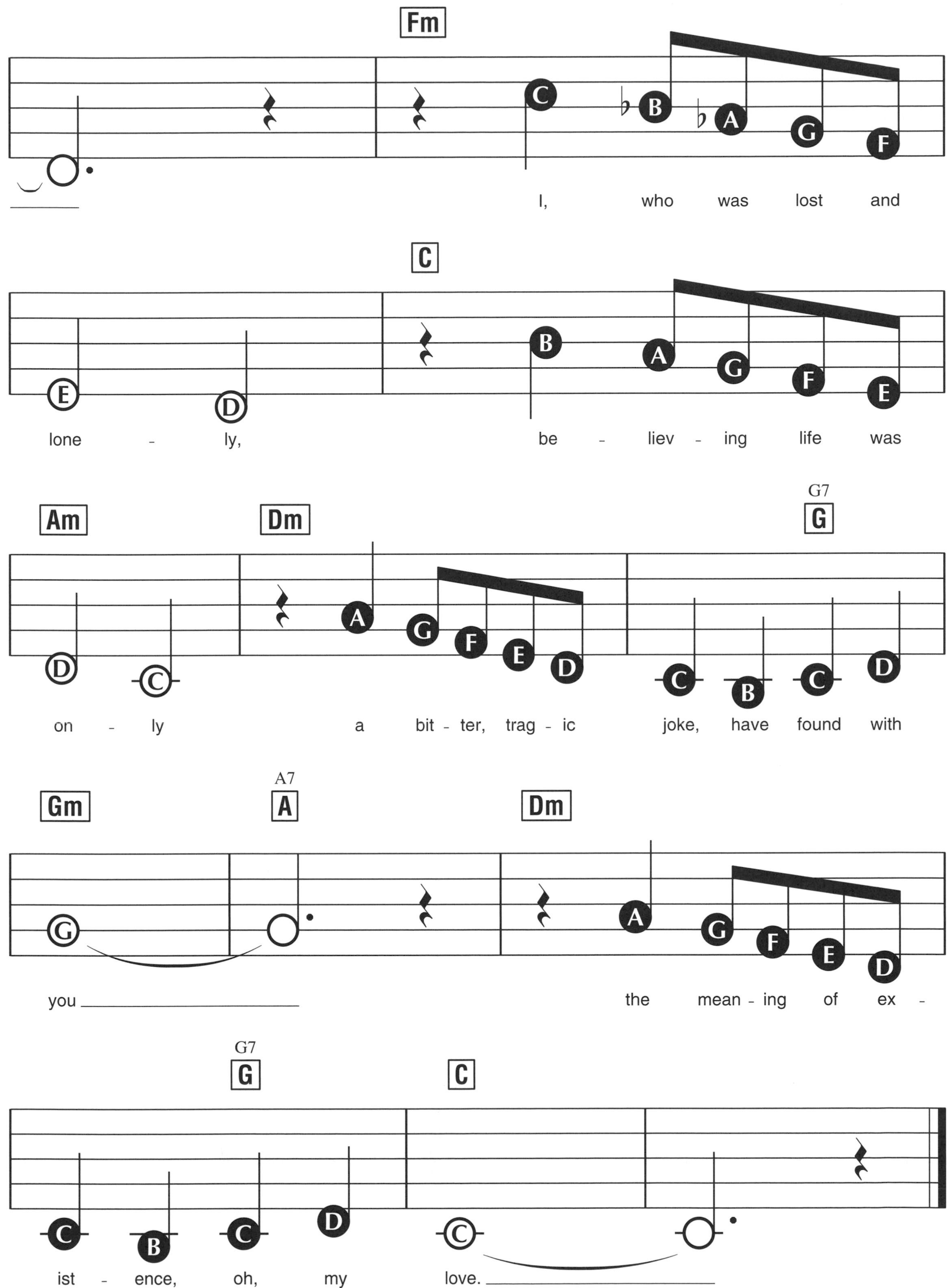
Fm
I, who was lost and
C
lone - ly,
be - liev - ing life was
Am
Dm
G7
G
on - ly
a bit - ter, trag - ic
joke, have found with
Gm
A7
A
Dm
you
the mean - ing of ex -
G7
G
C
ist - ence, oh, my
love.

Só Danço Samba
(Jazz 'n' Samba)

Registration 8
Rhythm: Samba or Latin

English Lyric by Norman Gimbel
Original Text by Vinicius de Moraes
Music by Antonio Carlos Jobim

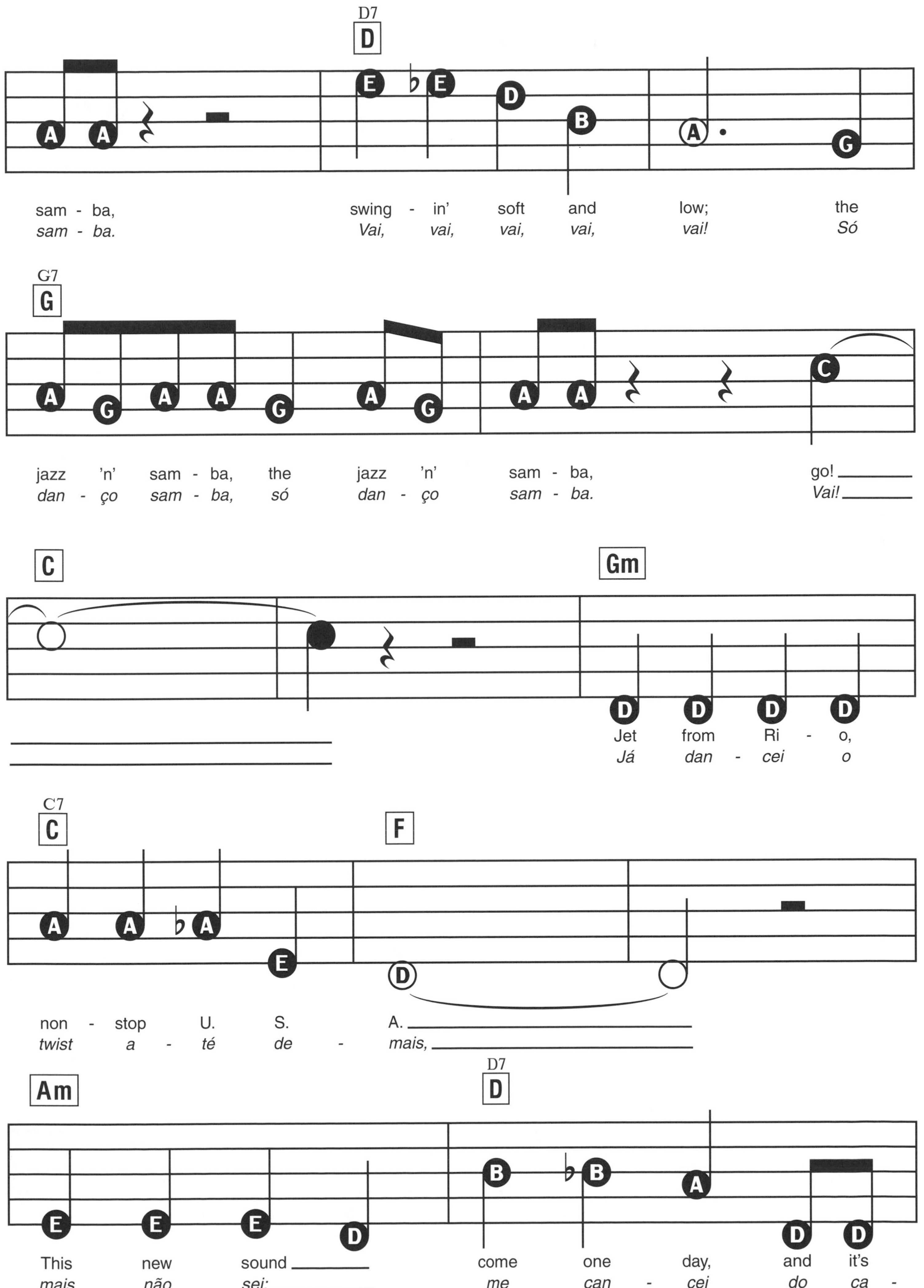
D7
D
sam - ba, swing - in' soft and low; the
sam - ba. Vai, vai, vai, vai, vai! Só
G7
G
jazz 'n' sam - ba, the jazz 'n' sam - ba, go!
dan - ço sam - ba, só dan - ço sam - ba. Vai!
C
Gm
Jet from Ri - o,
Já dan - cei o
C7
C
F
non - stop U. S. A.
twist a - té de - mais,
Am
D7
D
This new sound come one day, and it's
mais não sei; me can - cei do ca -

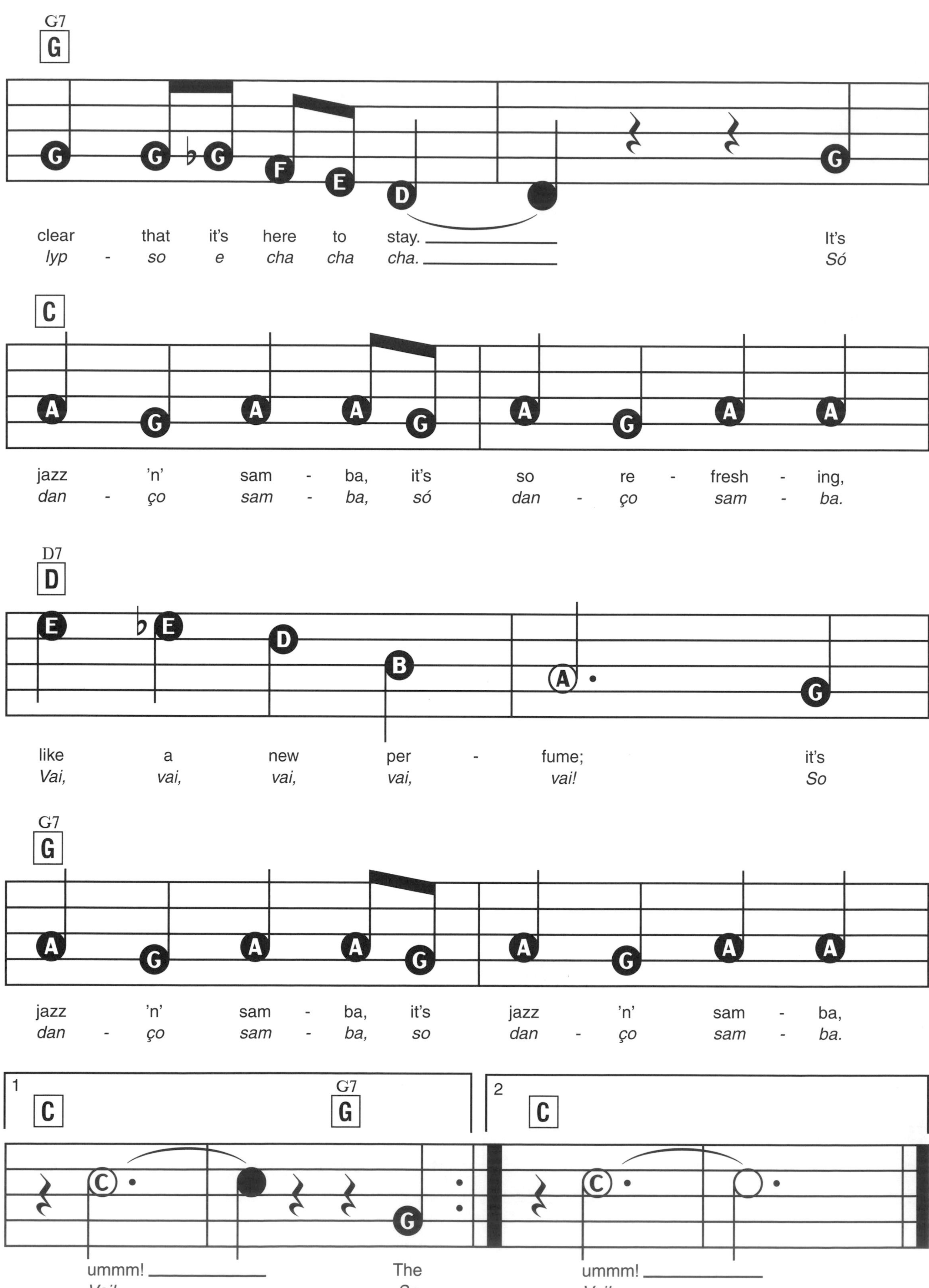
G7
G
clear that it's here to stay.
lyp - so e cha cha cha.
It's
Só
C
jazz 'n' sam - ba, it's so re - fresh - ing,
dan - ço sam - ba, só dan - ço sam - ba.
D7
D
like a new per - fume; it's
Vai, vai, vai, vai, vai! So
G7
G
jazz 'n' sam - ba, it's jazz 'n' sam - ba,
dan - ço sam - ba, so dan - ço sam - ba.
1
C
G7
G
ummm! The
Vai! So
2
C
ummm!
Vai!

Song of the Jet
(Samba do Avião)
from the film COPACABANA PALACE

Registration 2
Rhythm: Bossa Nova or Latin

English Lyric by Gene Lees
Original Text and Music by Antonio Carlos Jobim

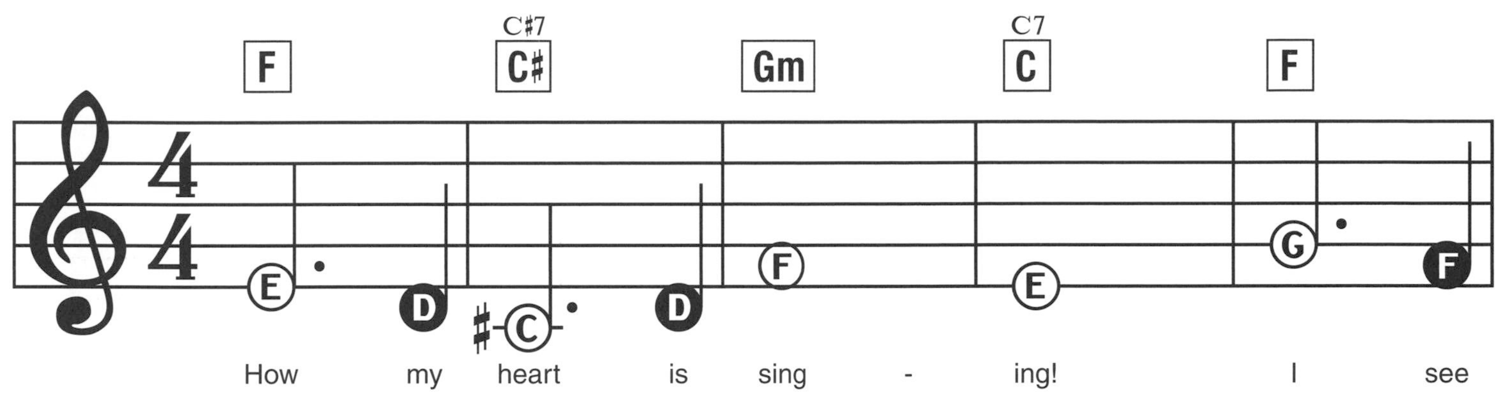

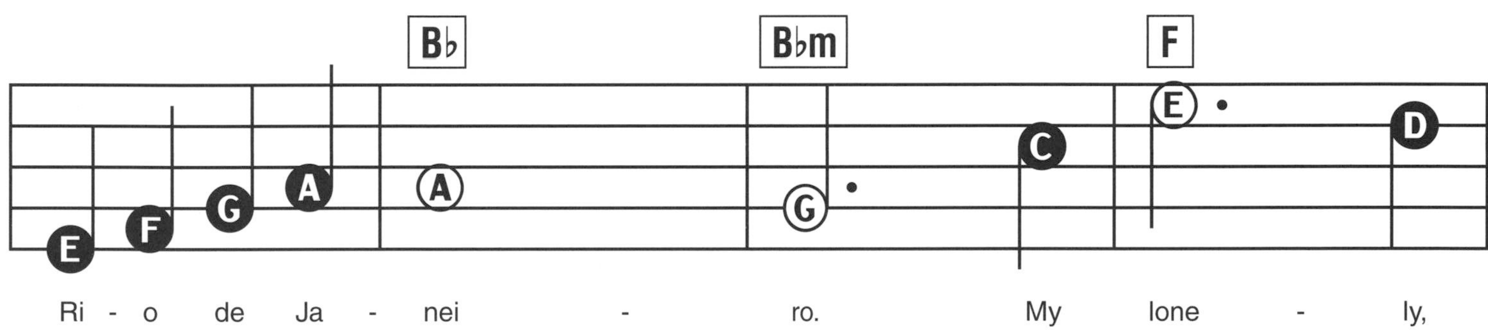

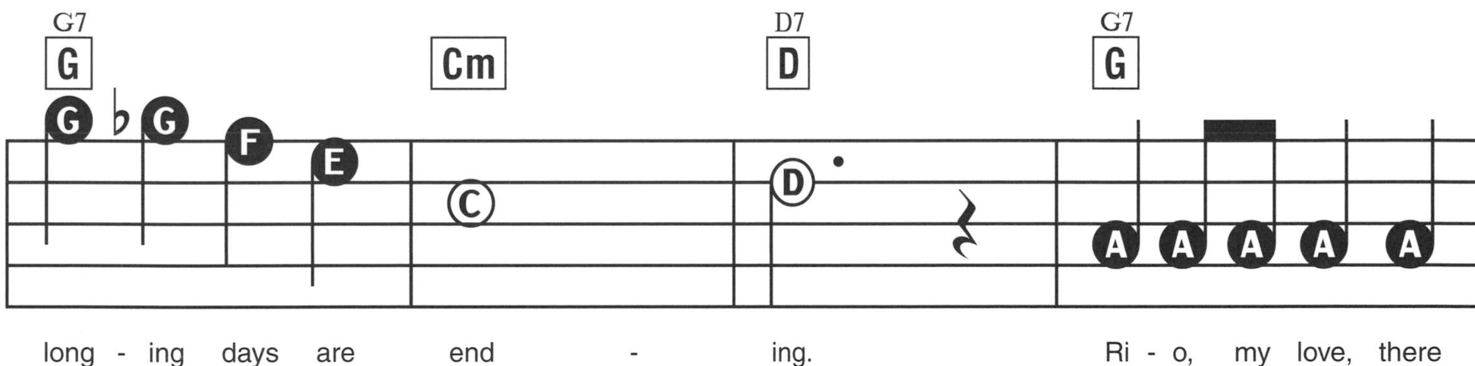

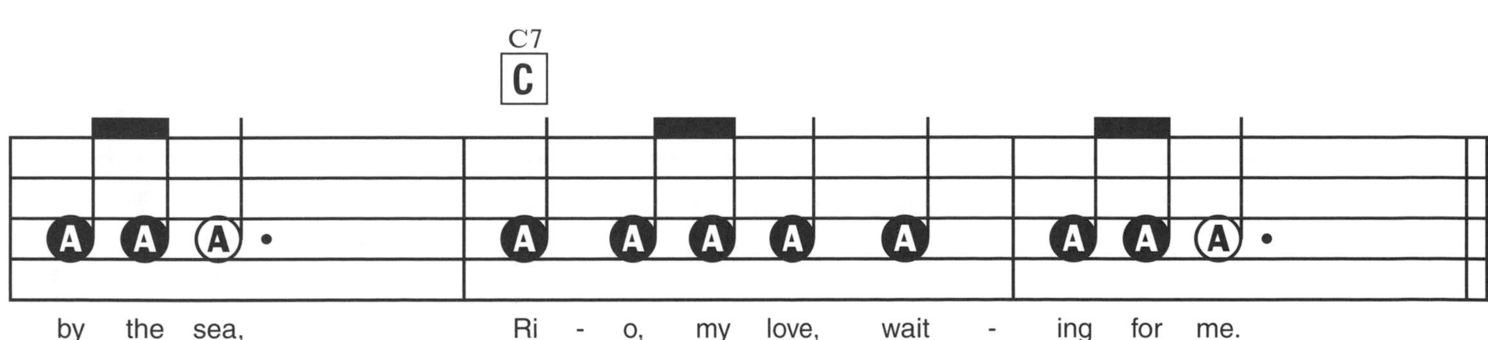

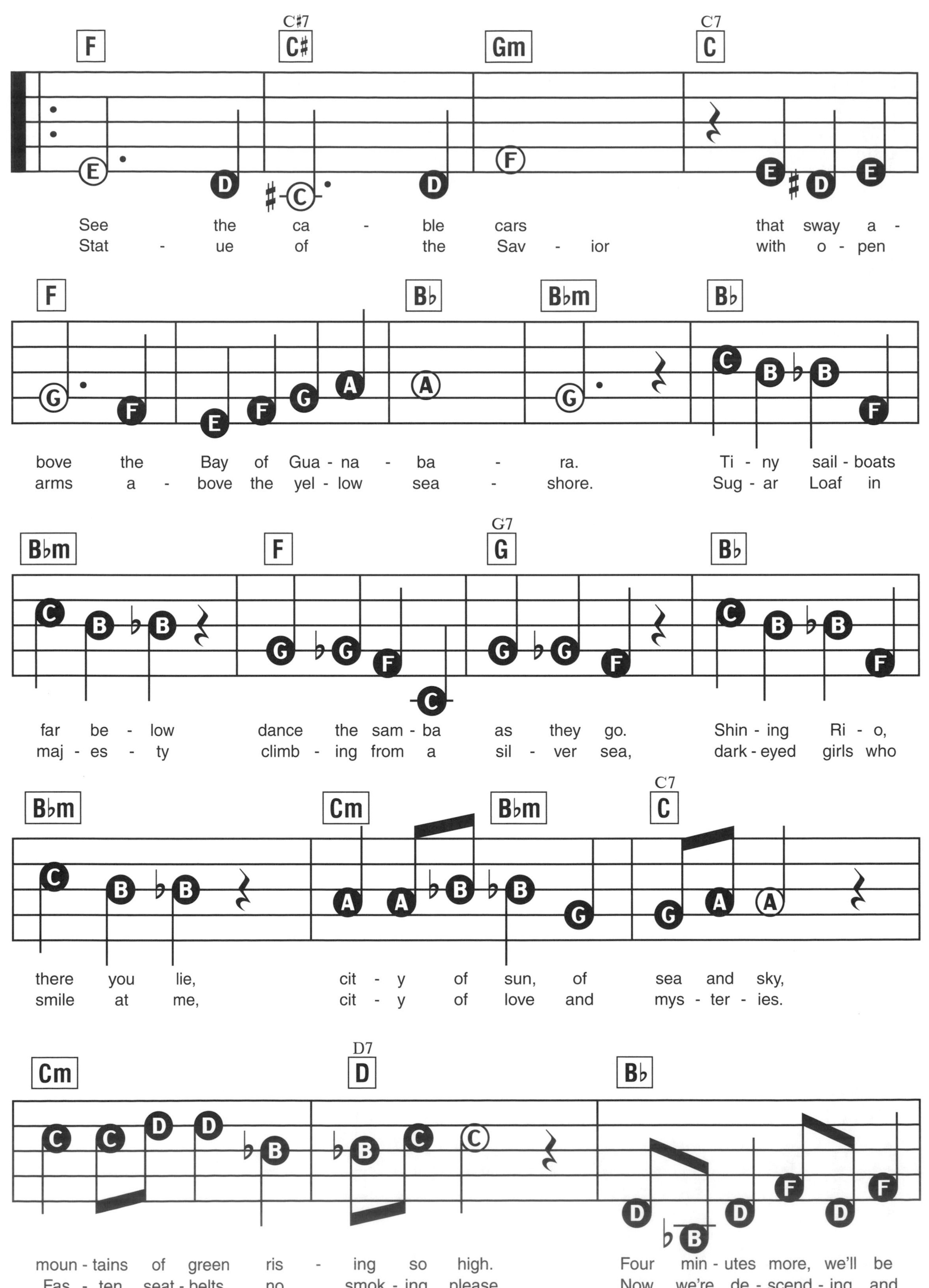
F C#7 C# Gm C7 C
See the ca - ble cars that sway a -
Stat - ue of the Sav - ior with o - pen
F Bb Bbm Bb
bove the Bay of Gua - na - ba - ra. Ti - ny sail - boats
arms a - bove the yel - low sea - shore. Sug - ar Loaf in
Bbm F G7 G Bb
far be - low dance the sam - ba as they go. Shin - ing Ri - o,
maj - es - ty climb - ing from a sil - ver sea, dark - eyed girls who
Bbm Cm Bbm C7 C
there you lie, cit - y of sun, of sea and sky,
smile at me, cit - y of love and mys - ter - ies.
Cm D7 D Bb
moun - tains of green ris - ing so high. Four min - utes more, we'll be
Fas - ten seat - belts, no smok - ing, please. Now we're de - scend - ing and

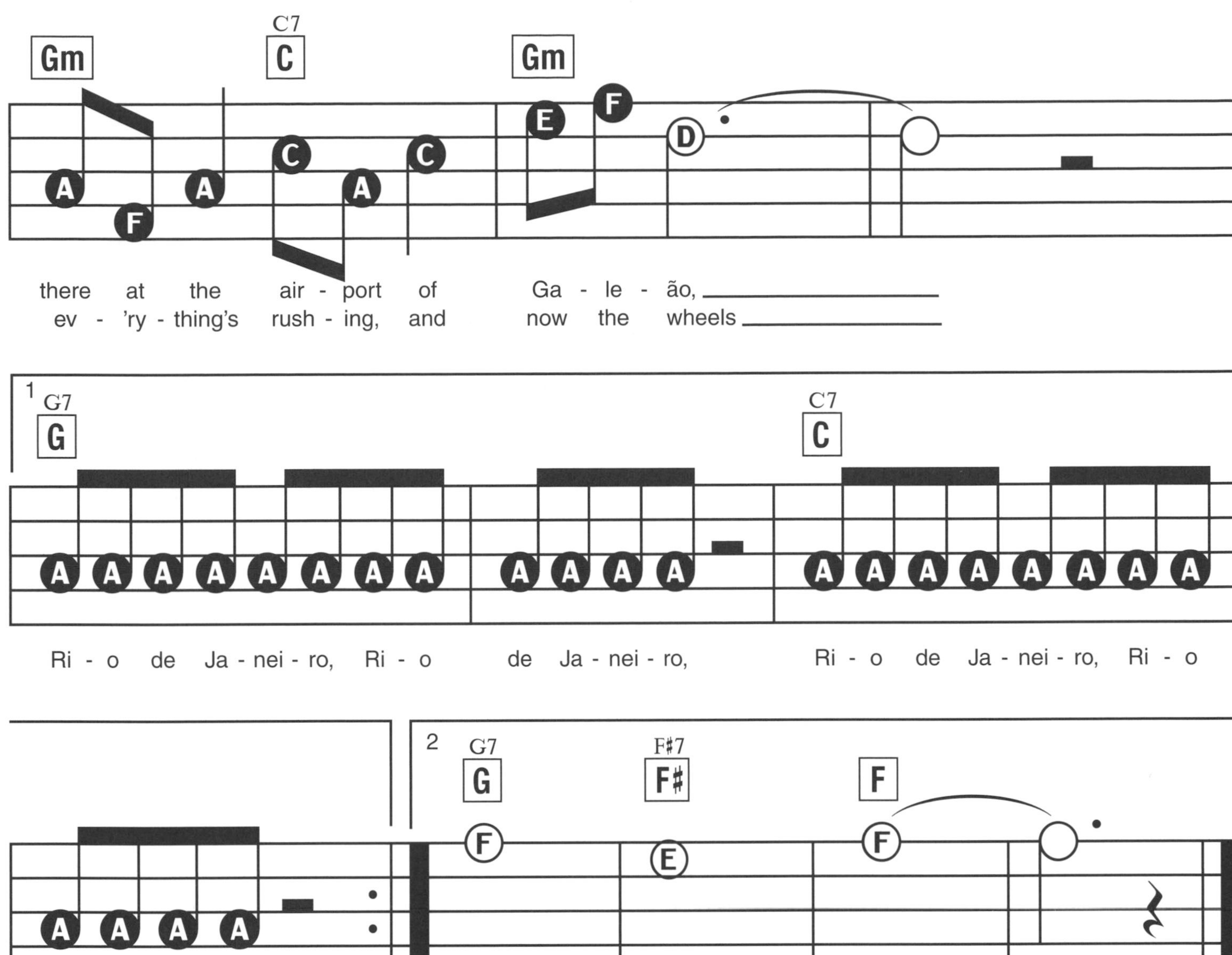

Portuguese Lyrics

Minha alma canta. Vejo o Rio de Janeiro.
Estou morrendo de saudade.
Rio, teu mar, praias sem fim,
Rio, você foi feito pra mim.
Cristo Redentor, braços abertos sobre a Guanabara.
Este samba é só porque,
Rio, eu gosto de você.
A morena vai sambar,
Seu corpo todo balançar.
Rio de sol, de céu, de mar,
Dentro de mais um minuto estaremos no Galeão.
Cristo Redentor, braços abertos sobre a Guanabara.
Este samba é só porque,
Rio, eu gosto de você.
A morena vai sambar,
Seu corpo todo banançar.
Aperte o cinto, vamos chegar.
Agua brilhando, olha a pista chegando,
E vamos nós,
Aterrar.

Triste

Registration 1
Rhythm: Bossa Nova or Latin

By Antonio Carlos Jobim

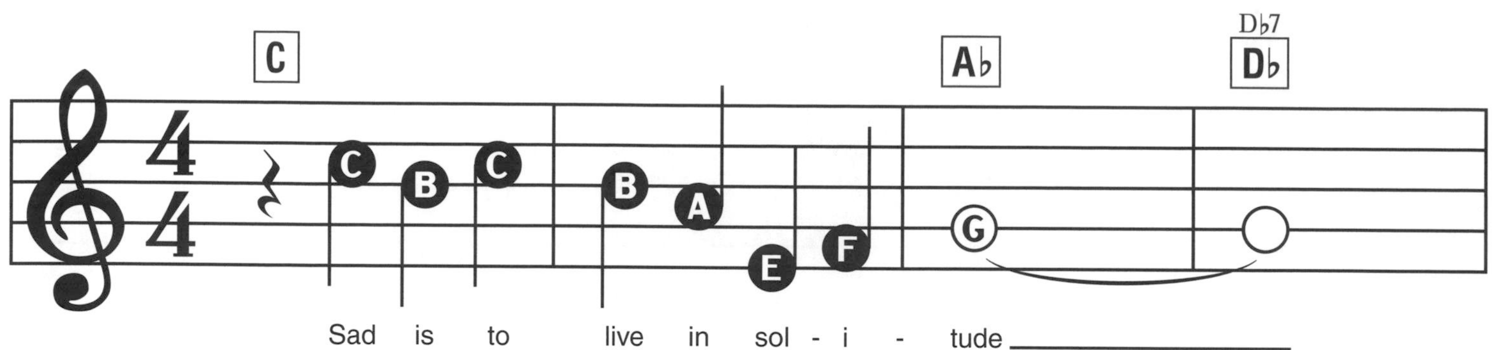

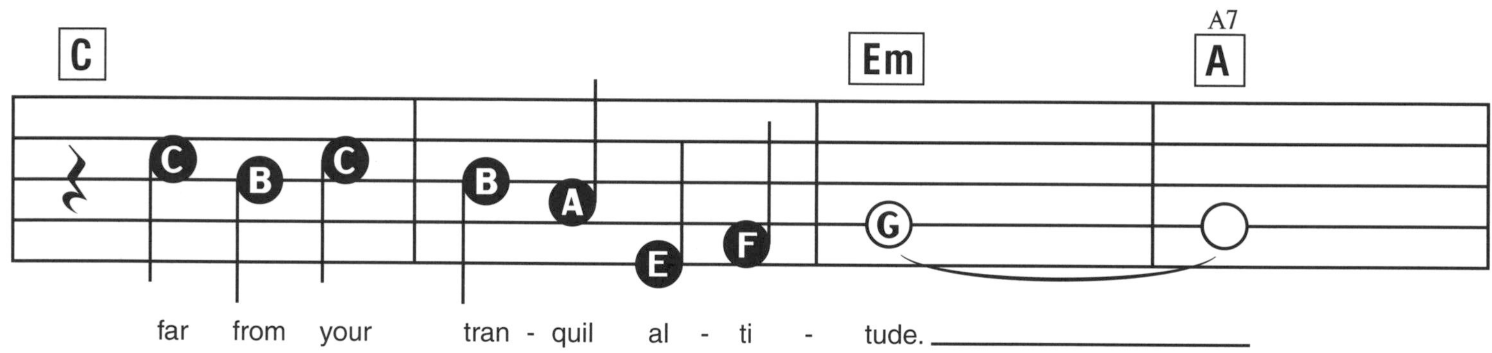

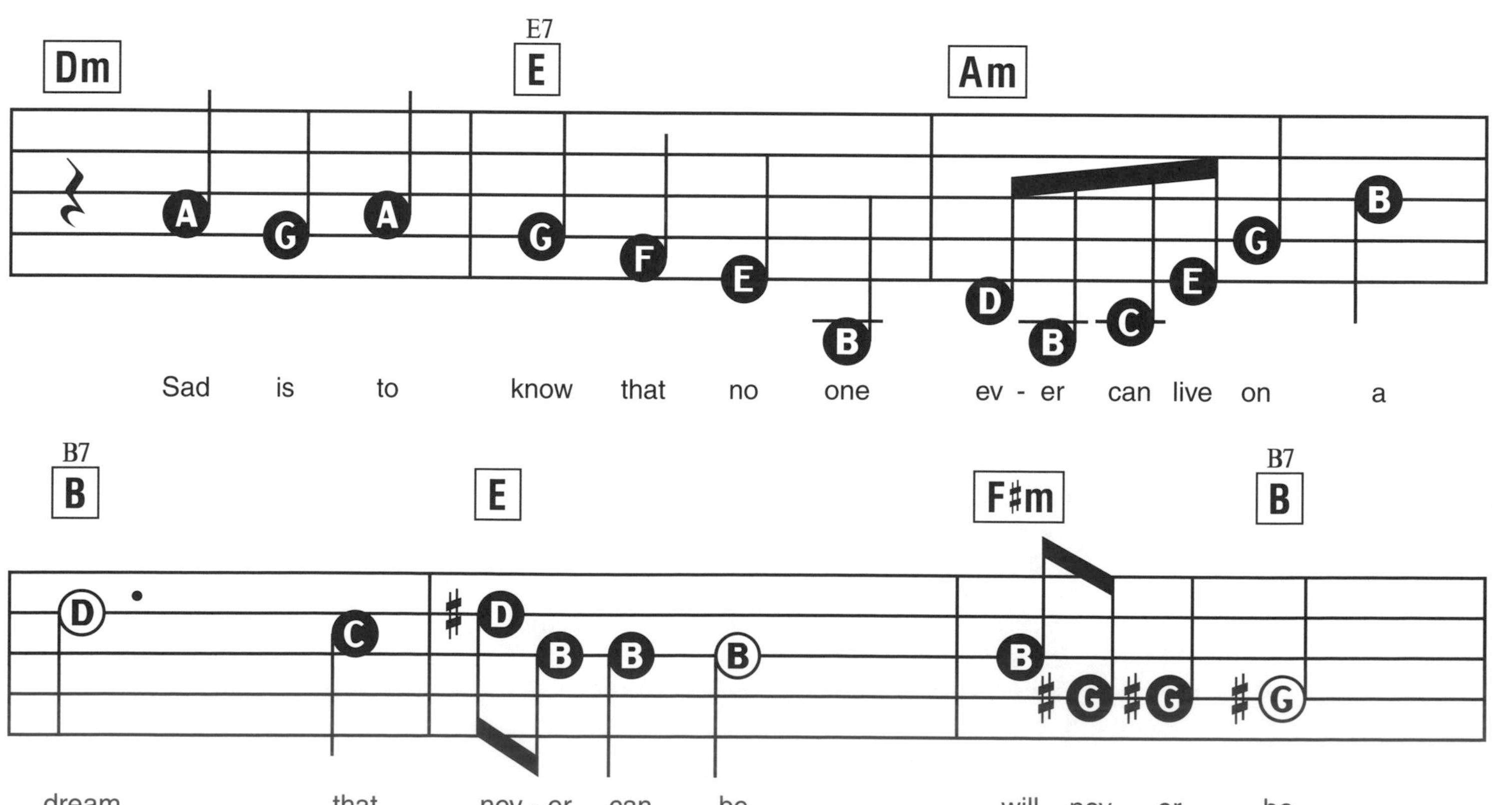

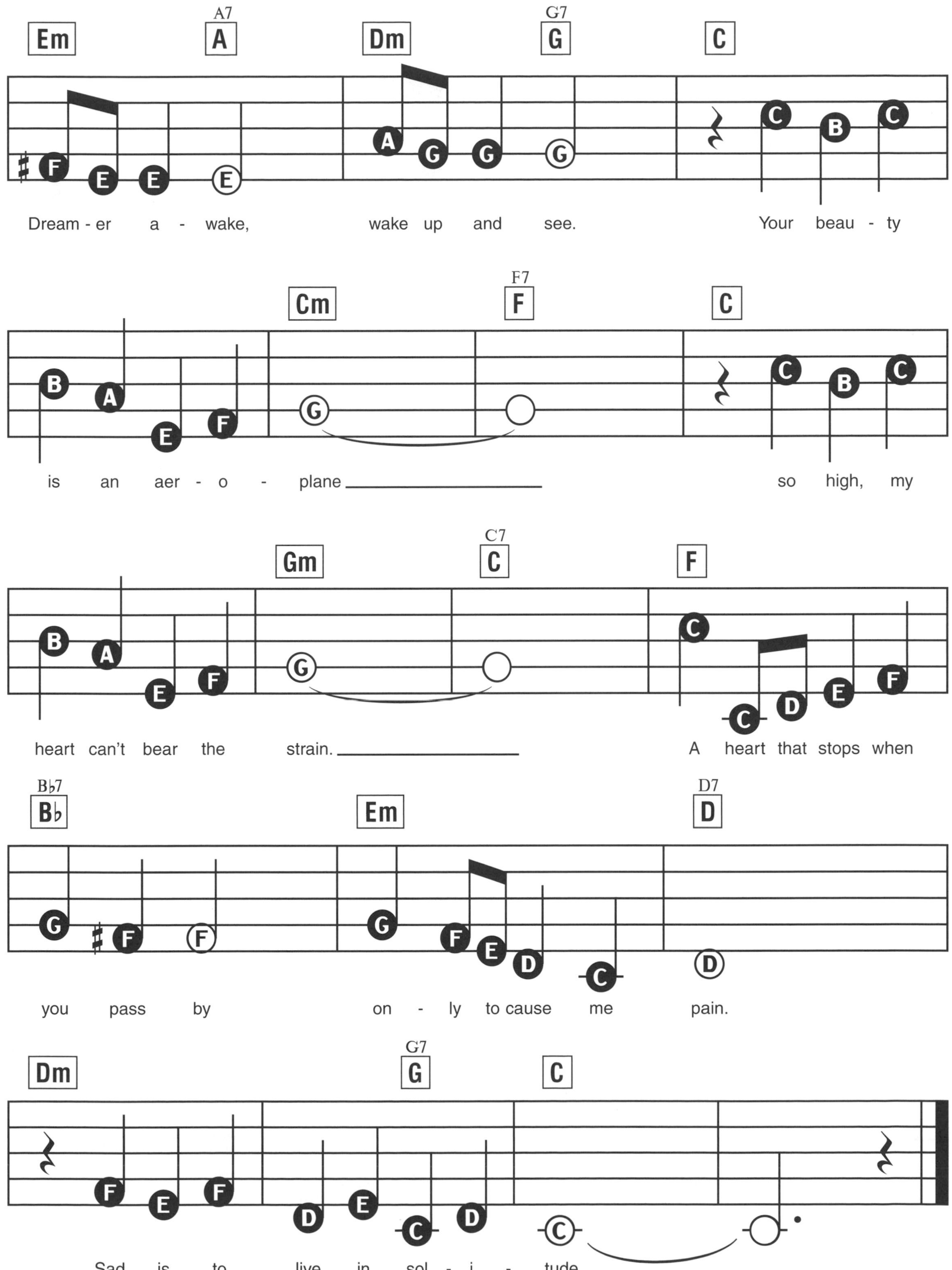
Em A7 A Dm G7 G C
Dream - er a - wake, wake up and see. Your beau - ty
Cm F7 F C
is an aer - o - plane so high, my
Gm C7 C F
heart can't bear the strain. A heart that stops when
B♭7 B♭ Em D7 D
you pass by on - ly to cause me pain.
Dm G7 G C
Sad is to live in sol - i - tude.

Wave

Registration 8
Rhythm: Bossa Nova or Latin

Words and Music by
Antonio Carlos Jobim

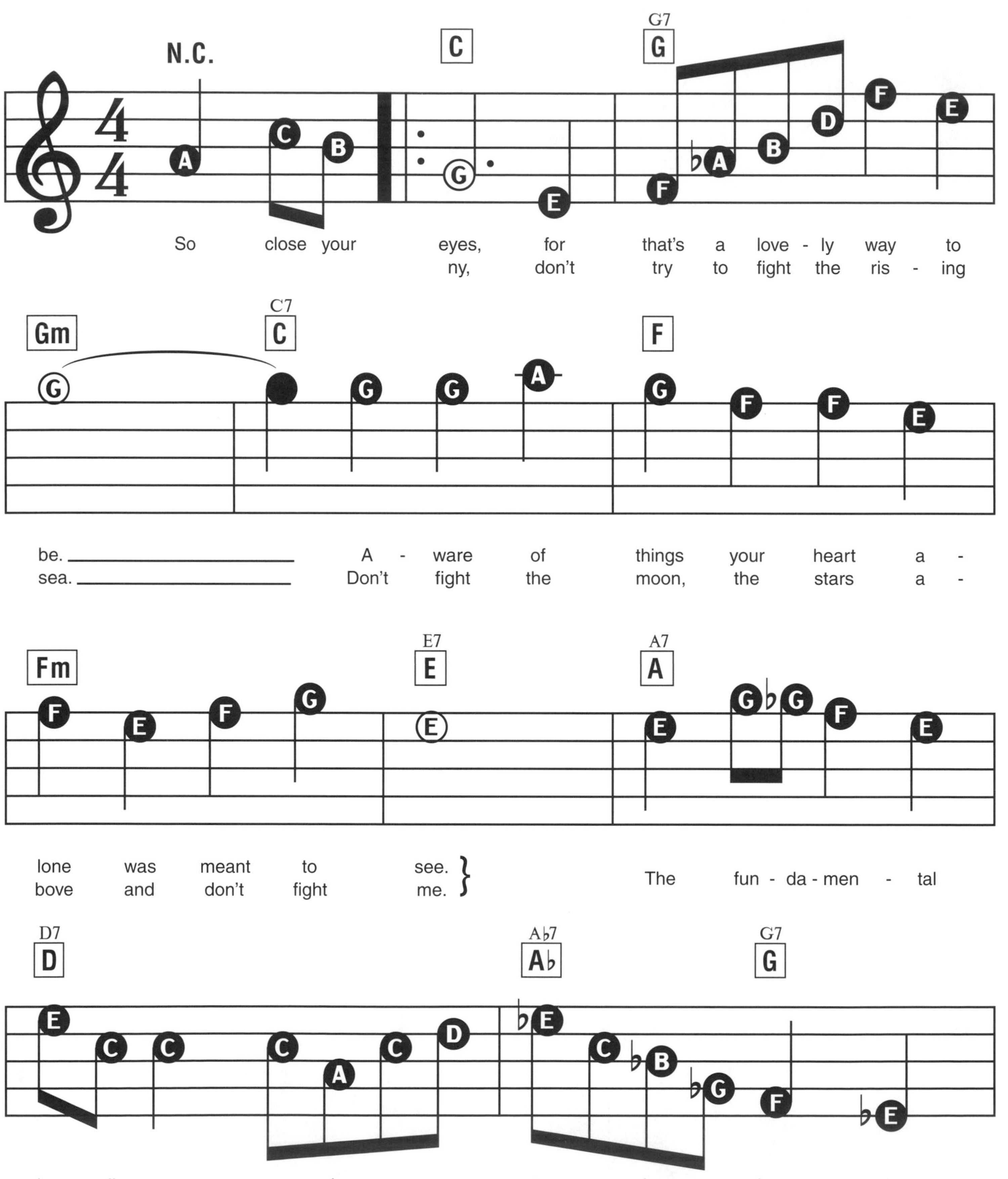

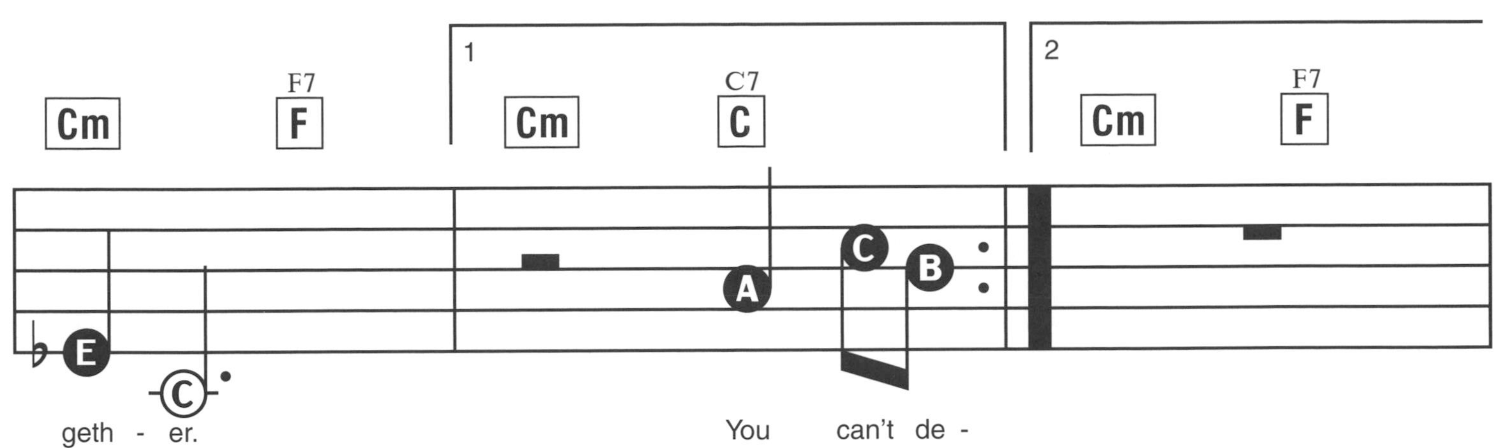
Cm
F7
F
1
Cm
C7
C
2
Cm
F7
F
geth - er.
You can't de -

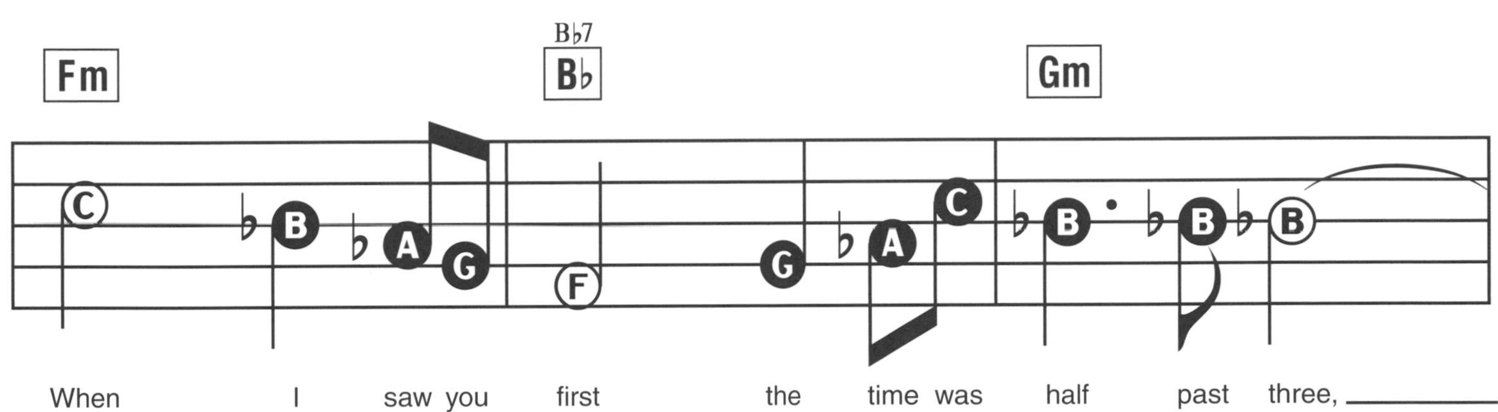
Fm
B♭7
B♭
Gm
When I saw you first the time was half past three,

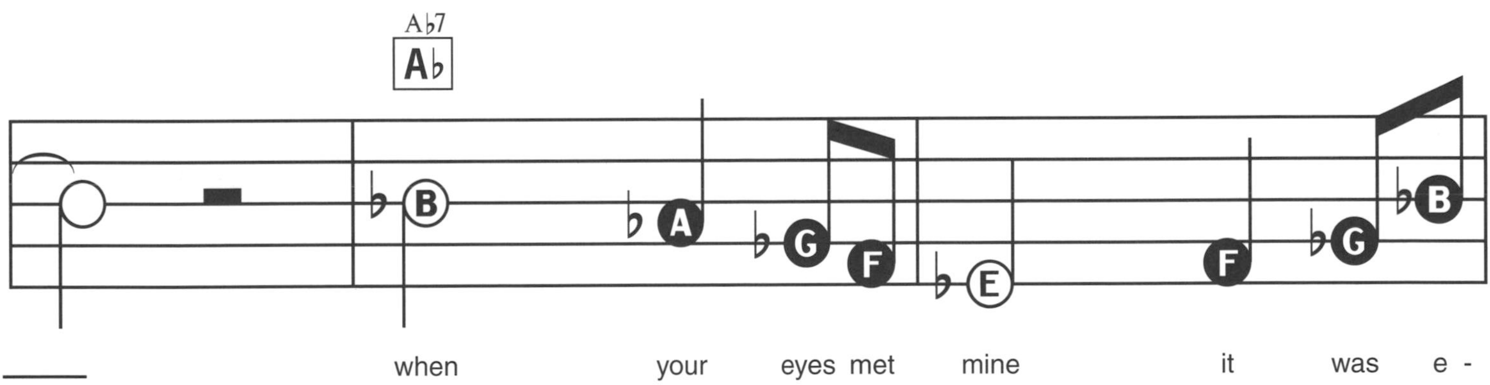
A♭7
A♭
when your eyes met mine it was e -

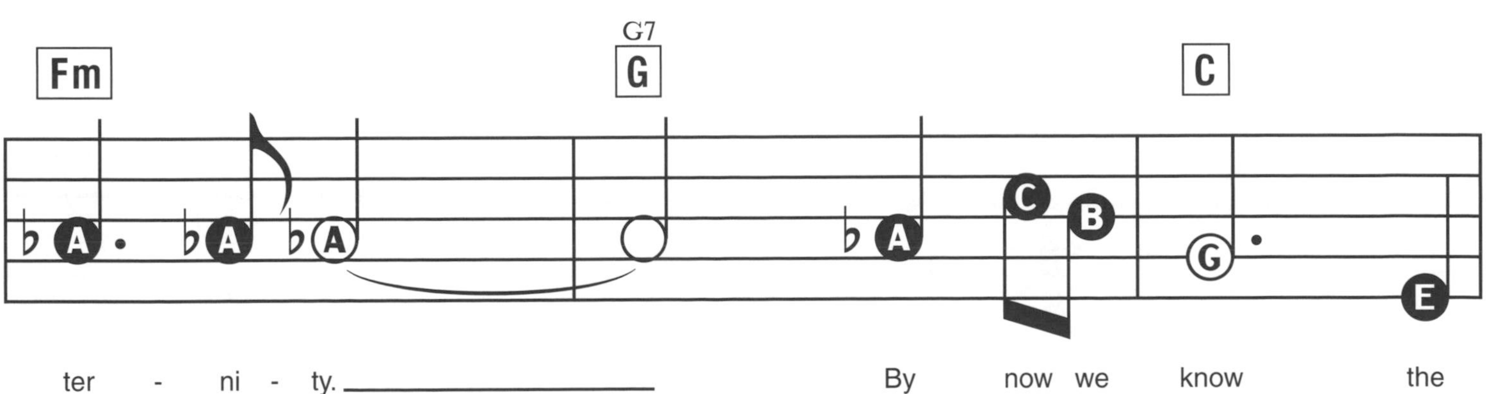
Fm
G7
G
C
ter - ni - ty.
By now we know the

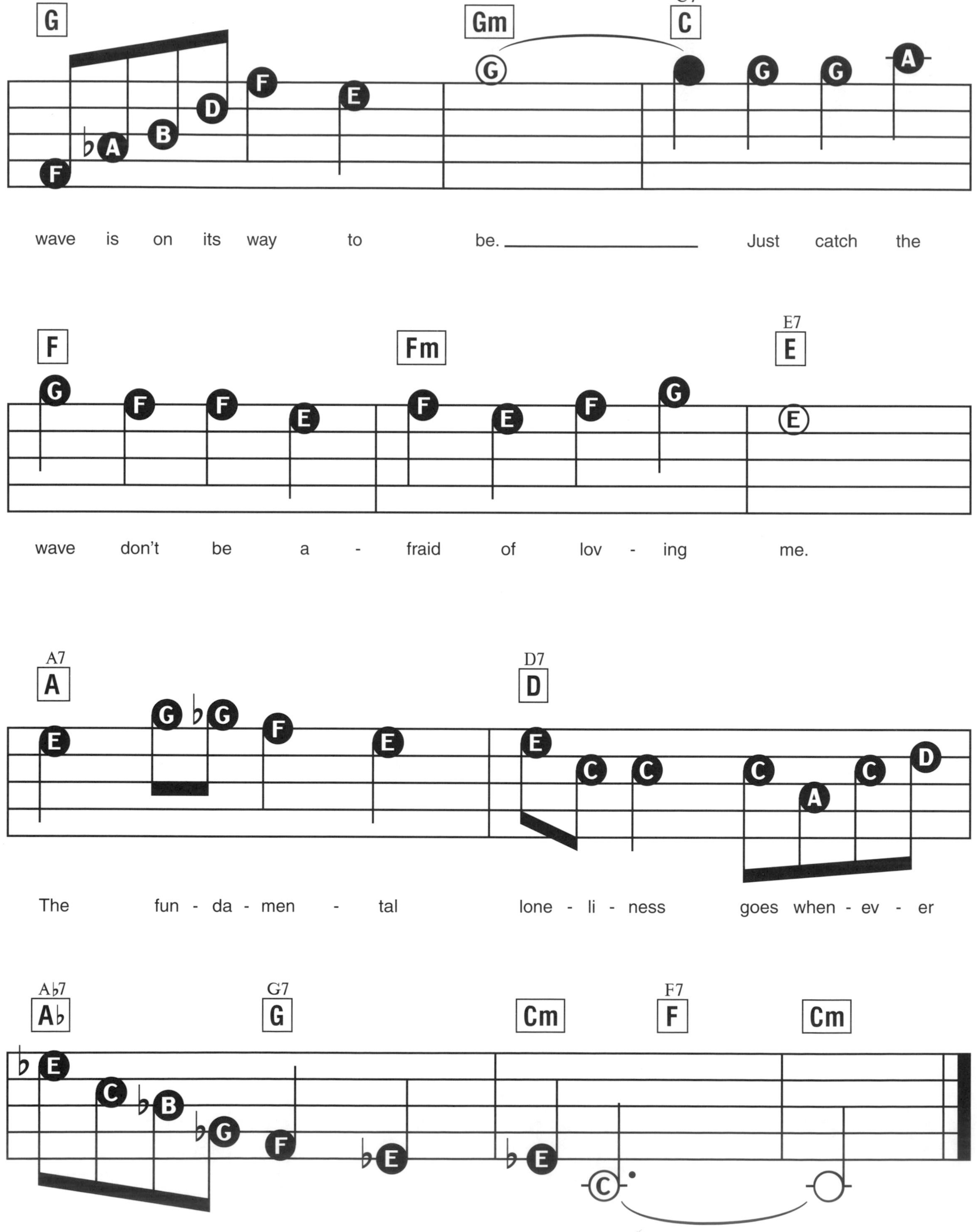
G7
G
Gm
C7
C
F
B♭A
B
D
F
E
G
G
G
A
wave is on its way to be. Just catch the
F
Fm
E7
E
G F F E F E F G E
wave don't be a - fraid of lov - ing me.
A7
A
D7
D
E G ♭G F E E C C C A C D
The fun - da - men - tal lone - li - ness goes when - ev - er
A♭7
A♭
G7
G
Cm
F7
F
Cm
♭E C ♭B ♭G F ♭E ♭E C
two can dream a dream to - geth - er.